Cry Until You Laugh

Cry Until You Laugh

Comforting Guidance for Coping with Grief

Richard J. Obershaw,
MSW, LICSW

Fairview Press   *Minneapolis*

Library of Congress Cataloging-in-Publication Data
Obershaw, Richard J., 1944–

    Cry until you laugh: comforting guidance for coping with grief / Richard J. Obershaw.

        p.   cm.

    Includes bibliographical references.

    ISBN 1-57749-063-0 (pbk. : alk. paper)

    1. Grief. 2. Bereavement—Psychological aspects. 3. Death—Psychological aspects. 4. Loss (Psychology) I. Title.

    BF575.G7024   1998

    155.9'3—DC21   97-27942

                                                        CIP

First Paperback Printing: 1992
First Hardcover Printing: 1997
Printed in the United States of America
02 01 00 99 98   7 6 5 4 3 2 1

Cover design: Laurie Duren

William Lamers' "Sequential Reaction to Loss" was taken from a lecture given to the Wisconsin Funeral Directors Association, 1966. It is reproduced with the author's permission.

Publisher's Note: The publications of Fairview Press, including Cry Until You Laugh, do not necessarily reflect the philosophy of Fairview Health System or its treatment programs. For a free current catalog of Fairview Press titles, please call this toll-free number: 1-800-544-8207, or visit our website at www.press.fairview.org.

This mixture of ideas, emotions, research, and history is dedicated to the following:

Mr. Ray J. (Penny) Eckstein, Mr. Clarence Novitzke, and Mr. John Werness, funeral directors that gave me the valuable opportunity to be close to the bereaved as a funeral director.

Dr. Robert Fulton, Dr. Elisabeth Kübler-Ross, and Mr. Charles Young, who ignited my desire to better understand and interact with the dying and the bereaved.

My family and friends, who encouraged this book; my professional staff, who worked the extra hours during this endeavor; and above all, the numerous patients who trusted me and shared their pain and recovery with me so I might learn to help others. They are the real experts!

CONTENTS

PREFACE

Death is one of the most difficult and profound experiences we must face. When a loved one dies, our identity and way of life change dramatically. We grieve. Although grief is both normal and healthy, the grief we experience when a loved one dies can seem intolerable at times.

Grief and loss are not limited to the death of a loved one. They may come from divorce, separation, disability, unemployment, and many other changes in life. Regardless of the source, the bereaved need our support as they try to work through their pain. Too often, though, grieving individuals are hurt by well-intentioned people who have unrealistic expectations about grief and healing.

This book is written for anyone who has suffered a loss. It is meant to help them clarify their experiences and redefine themselves in their time of grief. It is also written for friends and family of the bereaved who wish to understand and support them throughout the grieving process. Finally, professionals who confront grief and death in their work will appreciate the sensitive, practical advice this book offers.

I have tried to confront the expectations, myths, attitudes, and prejudices about grief that pervade our society. If you or someone you know is grieving, I hope you will come to see grief as a friend and ally that will remind you of the need to change and redefine yourself at every stage of life. If this book guides only one more person in that process, it has been well worth the effort.

Chapter One

UNDERSTANDING DEATH

At some point, we all must face death—the death of a hero, the death of an acquaintance, the death of a loved one, even our own death. Death is the only thing in life that is certain. All life eventually ends in death, but until we are dead, we are survivors. And as survivors of death, we are likely to experience grief.

To most of us, grief means pain and heartache. But the fact is, we incur loss every day, and we experience grief for each and every loss. Only by gaining a clear understanding of grief, by working through the grief and loss in our everyday lives, do we find the strength and knowledge we need to survive significant losses—death, divorce, or disability.

What is death? Who is dying? How does society view death? These are important questions, and when we explore the answers, we gain a greater understanding of this thing called grief.

What Is Death?

Defining death is not as easy as it might seem. The folks at Merriam-Webster tell us that death is "a permanent cessation of all vital functions." They refer us to the definition of brain death, which is "the final cessation of activity in the central nervous system, [especially] as indicated by a flat electroencephalogram (EEG) for a predetermined length of time."

You can imagine how important it is for staff at hospitals and morgues to have a precise and accurate definition of death. A group of lawyers and physicians worked months to write such a definition. The fifty-two-word definition they came up with could be summed up in just three words: "a flat EEG."

A number of years ago I was privileged to participate in a seminar with life-support and trauma unit professionals. The audience discussed donor organs, transplants, ethics, and the physiology of death.

A speaker posed the question, "When is a person dead?" Responses from the audience included: when all body functions cease, when there is no response to the environment, and when the person is not breathing and has no pulse. One member of the audience said, "Simple. When there are no brain waves."

The speaker projected a printout of an electroencephalogram, or EEG, on the overhead. The EEG was flat across most of the page, but, at the far right side, there was a minuscule bulge in the line. The speaker asked us if this EEG signified death. Someone in the audience replied, "No, that is not a flat EEG." The speaker declared, "Then please excuse me, I have to leave right away and call my colleagues back in Cleveland to tell them the bowl of Jell-O lives on!"

The speaker had projected an EEG of a bowl of Jell-O. He went on to show that there is no such thing as a flat EEG. He presented additional evidence, including a projection of an EEG taken in the desert. He showed that even sunspots can register on an EEG.

How do we know, then, if a person is dead? One of my favorite news articles on this topic came from a Boston newspaper. The headline read, "Two Survive after Hours of Frozen Death." The article told about a man found in the hallway of a Boston hotel who was sleeping off a "significant amount of liquor." When they found him, the man had no pulse and seemed, to all appearances, to be dead. Just two weeks earlier, in Winnipeg, Canada, a twenty-year-old woman had been found lying on a city street in the bitter cold. She had no heartbeat or respiration, and her pupils were dilated.

The reporter wrote, "While it took physicians over two-and-a-half hours to revive the man, and the woman's heart had stopped beating for over four hours, both victims are recovering with little evidence of any side effects."

The reporter went on to explain that seven doctors, ten nurses, and several orderlies worked on the woman for over three-and-a-half hours. They performed external heart massage and manual ventilation. Finally, they treated her with a technique known as peritoneal dialysis—the injection of a warm solution into the abdominal cavity. The woman regained consciousness and was able to talk and behave just like a person coming out of anesthesia. She recovered with no ill effects other than frostbite. At the end of the article, the reporter stated, "These unusual cases are causing authorities to again ponder the exact meaning of death."

I recently heard a story about a family who made burial arrangements for a relative who had died at a local hospital. Once the arrangements were made, the funeral director called the hospital to find out if the body could be released. A nurse told him that no one by that name had died. The funeral director was persistent, though he imagined the family could have given him the name of the wrong hospital. The nurse explained, "Oh, we have a patient here by that name, but he isn't dead yet."

Because the Federal Trade Commission was in the process of investigating funeral homes throughout the nation, the funeral director thought that maybe his establishment was being investigated, so he called a friend of his, an administrator at the hospital.

"I might have a big problem here," the funeral director began. He went on to tell about the family who had come into his funeral home to make arrangements for their relative. The family had said that the relative had died at this hospital, but a nurse had told him, "Nope. No one dead here by that name."

The administrator confirmed that the person was there, but he wasn't really dead yet.

The funeral director asked, "What do you mean, not really dead yet? The family didn't say this was a pre-arrangement. They said that their husband and father had died."

"Well," the administrator replied, "he's being kept alive on life support. But please don't tell the family." The first recipient for the patient's donor organs hadn't made it to the hospital, so staff was waiting for a second recipient to be found.

The funeral director waited until the next morning before calling his friend again. "Look, I need that body," he began. "The family is coming in at noon, and they have no idea. . . ." The administrator apologized, but maintained that the person wasn't really dead yet. The funeral director called the family to explain why the body of their loved one would not be at the funeral home that day. The family became upset and eventually sued the hospital. The suit was partly a response to their attempts to answer difficult questions: When do we know that our loved one is dead? When do we begin our grief?

When is a person dead? becomes an especially pertinent question in this day and age, because there are more and more grandmas and grandpas and husbands and wives and fathers and mothers attached to machines to keep them alive.

Who is Dying?

Perhaps we can better answer the question, "When is a person dead?" when we come to a clear understanding of who is actually dying in society today.

The answer is in the evidence: the bodies in a cemetery. When a body is buried, you can be pretty sure it was pronounced dead first.

If you go to a historical cemetery, you will find many infant graves. Back in the early to mid-1900s, children often died of illnesses for which no cures were known. Given the progress of today's medical technology, you would expect that fewer and fewer children would be dying in our society. However, the media would have us believe that an extraordinarily high percentage of children are dying. The news tells of kids dying on the streets from drug abuse, gang violence, teenage suicide, even from murder. We are concerned—and rightfully so, if these accounts are accurate.

But our perception of fact has become shaded by sensationalism. People have always attempted to profit from other people's fears. To argue the points of sensationalism and profiteering in today's news media would take an entire book, and I won't dwell on the topic here. However, it is important to note that our perception—that children make up a large percentage of the dying in our society— probably doesn't take into account the whole story, which includes a decreased infant mortality rate due to advances in medical technology. Today we see fewer stillbirths than ever before, as well as higher survival rates for premature babies.

I get alarmed when people believe that a few pertinent facts comprise the whole story, especially when the topic is as complex as death. Of course, it doesn't matter what the topic is, one can always find statistics to support an opinion. When statistics are presented, we are often shown only a small, grim segment of a much wider, more compelling horizon. We are misled, and unfounded fears result.

While statistics suggest that youth make up a high percentage of people dying today, funeral directors—the people who see dead bodies before they are buried—will say that no matter what you hear, more than 65% of all deaths are elderly people (over the age of sixty-five). When you see the statistics on children who die from gang violence, drug abuse, and suicide, don't believe that we live in a society where children have a greater chance of dying than their parents. The fact is, people get old, people get sick, and every person on the face of this earth will eventually die. It's always been that way, and it always will be.

The elderly make up the largest percentage of the people dying. And the largest percentage of those dying are doing so in hospitals and hospice centers, not in their homes.

How Does Society View Death?

There are times when what we say is different from what we do. We send and receive mixed messages, and in doing so, we perpetuate an inaccurate (and often unhealthy) understanding of a topic. Mixed messages can further confuse and obscure an already unclear issue. The topic of death is a prime example.

I am frequently invited to speak to high school students. Each time a dean or administrator introduces me, the introduction goes something like this: "Today, we are very privileged to have Mr. Obershaw as our guest presenter. He is going to help us learn how to cope when someone we know and love passes away." Then my job is to clear up the mistaken impression that people "pass away." People don't "pass away," they die.

Of course, we have all had mistaken impressions at one time or another. I grew up in a small town in Wisconsin. In my sophomore year of high school, we had a sex education class. The instructor for the class was a very young, very pretty first-year teacher. She couldn't have been more than twenty-two years old. When she stood up at the front of the room, everyone recognized her as the driver education instructor. Here, the same teacher who had taught us our behind-the-wheel skills was going teach us about sex! You can imagine the giggles from us guys sitting at the back of the room. There we were, imagining that sex had something to do with cars. And the poor instructor stood nervously at the front of the class and assured us, "Now, there's no reason for any of you to be laughing! Sex is a normal and natural topic." Yet she was showing us how abnormal and unnatural she felt just teaching the subject.

We got two very different messages that morning. The first was that driving and sex somehow went together, and to us that was funny. The second was that sex is a serious subject, that there is no reason to laugh about sex. Well, to us, it was a big joke. Here we were, impressionable, young kids who imagined that we would graduate from that class with our license to have sex. Sure, it's not so funny now, especially when we consider that our kids could be getting mixed messages, too.

We give and receive similarly mixed messages about death. Go to a nursing college that teaches specialized care to would-be hospice nurses. Ask the administration what they teach students about grief and bereavement, about surviving death. You will find that these schools have limited curriculums on this topic.

Funeral directors and other grief experts know that the funeral is really for the living, not for the dead. But during a funeral, they hide the family in a secluded room to grieve. Where will the bereaved get support? From each other? Not likely.

Members of the clergy often tell us that we've got to deal with the reality of death. And then they preach about the dead having to "cut loose from the moorings on the ship of life." Throughout the funeral service, they may not even mention the fact that someone died.

Hospitals pay me well to teach their staff how to communicate with dying patients, deal with death and grieving, and help the bereaved. Yet they hide one of the very best communicators of death—the dead body. Some even go to the extreme of hiding dead bodies in carts with false bottoms. This is absurd, especially since the majority of deaths in America occur in health care institutions. It shows how society continues to send mixed messages about death.

There has been more written in the past fifteen to twenty years about death, dying, grief, and bereavement than at any other time in our history. Unfortunately, much of what has been written confuses rather than clarifies. After twenty years, our discussions of death and dying have not changed.

Even in prominent hospice centers and terminal-care facilities, staff can't say the words "dead" or "died." They can't talk about their fears of death with other staff members, let alone with patients or survivors.

Death as Weird, Unbelievable, and in Bad Taste

I don't doubt that many of you have seen the TV series M*A*S*H. If, by some slim chance, you have never seen an episode, you need to know that about 80% of it is humorous and 20% is serious. And the serious part is *very* serious. M*A*S*H is the story of a medical unit in Korea during the Korean War. At one point in the series, one of the major characters—Henry Blake, played by McLean Stevenson—is killed.

Mr. Stevenson decided to contract with another TV network to do a different series, so the producers had to write him out of the script. Like most major TV characters who wish to leave a show, Stevenson was written out by being killed off. You may recall the death of the character Edith in *All in the Family*. And when the character of Bobby Ewing on *Dallas* talked about leaving the show, he was killed off in a season finale. Of course, when the actor changed his mind, the character's death ended up to be "just a dream."

What I want you to understand and appreciate is that all of these deaths are just "TV deaths." When Henry Blake was no longer going to be a part of M*A*S*H, he was written out of the script through death—it was a fantasy death, an entertainment death. It wasn't the real death of a real person.

You'd think this character's death would have had little or no effect on us as viewers. After all, we knew the character wasn't real. But his death affected us greatly. As fans, we had invested much of ourselves in the characters on the show. Whenever we invest in something and then lose it, we have to divest ourselves of that thing. We grieve, and we must then work through that grief.

Right after the episode in which Col. Blake was "killed," a large city newspaper ran a story headlined "Viewers Blast TV Death." The article stated, "Switchboards at CBS glowed an angry red last week when Col. Henry Blake was killed off during the final moments of the show. A source at the Hollywood studio that produces the show said the reaction to the sad ending was 'tremendous.' The networks across the country were jammed with calls, and viewers were reportedly generally upset that Blake had been killed." It went on to say that a Los Angeles TV talk-show host went on the air and threatened to "beat up the persons responsible for Blake's demise." One network channel logged more that forty angry calls in just one hour, because of "the weird, unbelievable, and bad-taste conclusion to what had been an entertaining episode."

If you look at the response to what was only a TV death—for the purpose of entertainment—and multiply it several times, you begin to get an idea of how real death is viewed and responded to in our society today. In a nutshell, we see death as weird, unbelievable, and in bad taste, instead of what it really is—normal, natural, and highly desirable.

Death as Practical

To understand death, we must first look at the practicalities. After all, don't some of us take things too darned seriously in this day and age? Isn't part of the reason we have so many problems in society because we get "too emotional" over things? If we could eliminate our emotions and come to a clearer, more practical understanding of death, we'd be better off as survivors.

Let's take a look at the casket. There are a lot of emotional reasons for a casket, but let's disregard those for a moment. Can you imagine any practical uses for a casket? One, a casket is stronger than a canvas bag. But a canvas bag is more practical from an economic standpoint, as caskets can get pretty expensive. A casket does protect a loved one's body, but that's too emotional. Let's try to keep it practical.

A casket has handles, and that's practical. A container with handles makes it easier to carry. That's probably the only practical reason for caskets. Sure, caskets can be locked, but unless you believe the dead need to protect the jewelry or other valuables buried with them, locks on caskets serve no practical purpose. It could take six or eight people to carry a body from the funeral home to the hearse to the burial site, so caskets with handles are practical.

Society would have us get even more practical about caskets. It encourages us to purchase our caskets ahead of time so we can save the trouble and increased expense we would otherwise incur at some point in the future. As if we'll be there at the time of our death to worry about such matters.

I've spent some time thinking about this, and I honestly don't think there is anything I could buy today—even a casket—that I could take with me when I die. After all, dead is dead.

How can we make death practical? From an economic standpoint, we could measure the cost of a death. For instance, if someone dies in a car accident today, that death costs over $1,000,000! I will itemize this to make it sound more practical: $741,370 in loss of production and consumption in the marketplace; $222,407 in loss to the home, family, and community; $963 for the hospital; $560 for doctors; $455 for the coroner; $3,272 for the funeral; $7,665 for legal expenses; $1,032 for handling insurance claims; $280 for accident investigation; $12,897 in losses to others; $13,965 in car damages; and finally, $280 for delaying traffic.

Okay, that sounds practical. But society would not have us stop here. In many places you can immortalize your loved one, friend, or acquaintance by molding their cremated ashes into pottery. Really, they can be made into pottery! You can have flower pots and sculptures made out of your loved ones' remains.

Think about it. Practical. A pot keeps on being. It doesn't waste space. And a hundred years from now it will be a valuable family heirloom. An artist in a southern state says, "It's better to be looking out on the world as a pot, than to be buried under the wet, cold ground." A young farm kid from Wisconsin suggested to his mother that his hard-driving father could be molded into the shape of a foot scraper when he died. I'm sure that kid paid for his recklessness.

Now, if death is to be practical, we certainly can't have the dead take up space. That's not practical! At least, the United States government doesn't think so. A few years ago, members of our government became worried about all the valuable space being wasted on cemeteries, so they formed a committee to discuss what should be done about it. There was a strong faction suggesting that cemeteries should be done away with completely because they are just not practical.

Have you ever been to Washington, D.C.? Most of that city is one huge cemetery. Everywhere you look, you can see a marker or monument to the dead. If we were to do away with space for the dead, we would have to bulldoze the whole city.

The real reason people want to do away with cemeteries has nothing to do with wasted space or practical issues. Research shows that if everyone alive in the United States died today, the bodies could be buried in a space one-quarter of the size of our smallest state, Rhode Island. Those of you who have traveled to North Dakota know that there's enough land out there to bury bodies for hundreds of years to come. (If you're reading this in North Dakota, imagine Iowa.)

No, society does not wish to move cemeteries for practical reasons. We would like to move our cemeteries because we think death is weird, unbelievable, and in bad taste. We don't understand it. We cannot overcome it. We are afraid of death.

Could you get to heaven faster if you were cremated? Perhaps. A while back, our government approved a plan to send cremated human remains into outer space. The newspaper headline read, "You Can Go to Heaven When You Die." In smaller print below, it read, "Or at Least to the Heavens."

The article stated that by 1987, it would cost about $3,900 per participant for a Florida-based consortium of funeral directors and engineers to orbit a flying mausoleum containing cremated remains. It was the first time the Department of Transportation had given approval to a private business to launch a commercial spacecraft.

This spacecraft-mausoleum was to carry 10,330 lipstick-sized titanium capsules, each containing the specially reduced ashes of a cremated person. The mausoleum was to be placed in the nose cone of a privately developed rocket and fired into a circular orbit 1,900 miles above the earth. The orbit was said to be stable enough to keep the remains aloft for "at least 63 million years, if not for eternity."

It's difficult for cemeteries or funeral homes to obtain zoning permits in most communities, so funeral directors in Florida hired engineers and came up with an orbiting mausoleum. The projected orbit extended into the Van Allen (radiation) belt. There would be no problems for society: out of sight is out of mind. There are no inhabitants to worry about out there, so there would be no need for hearings and zoning permits. Now, that's practical!

But even more practical was a letter sent to a financial columnist in a large Midwestern city a few years ago. A reader, considering the practicalities of death, wrote that his wife was being kept alive by machines in a hospital. The doctors said she could be kept alive for another two months. That meant she would not die until the following year. The writer wondered, "If I decide to let them continue life-support, and she doesn't die until next year, what difference will that make on my income tax return? . . . Would I still get to deduct her?" Practical, very practical.

Even a national foundation that fights organ disease would have us make death more practical. Recently, the foundation ran a radio ad: "Ladies and gentlemen, did you know that last year, approximately two million people died in our United States? (*Rising music*) Two million people! That means four million lungs [kidneys, etc.] or two million hearts [livers, etc.] were buried needlessly and wastefully. Friends, donate your organs. Sign your donor cards today!" (*Music, up and out.*)

Maybe you have seen the TV ad I call the "practically dead ad." The ad cautions viewers, "Don't drink and drive." It is shot from the perspective of a drunken driver who has driven recklessly into a fatal accident. The dead driver is looking up from an open grave at his or her weeping family. A shovel of dirt is thrown in over the camera lens. The implication is terrible: if you drink and drive, you could get killed. But you won't actually be dead; you'll still be able to look out of the grave.

You can do something foolish and end up in a grave, but you won't be dead. In fact, you will still be around to see your family mourn. What does this suggest to one who is contemplating suicide? Some people want to commit suicide, in part, to inflict emotional and physical pain on those closest to them. They also want to relieve the intense pain they feel themselves. And here's an advertisement that suggests that when you die, you won't actually be D-E-A-D dead. Death will not be as painful or as alone as you might imagine it to be. And all these people who are close to you will mourn your passing. As an added bonus, you'll be able to watch!

Since suicide doesn't really mean D-E-A-D dead, the distraught teenager can get her family's attention, the jilted lover can get his revenge, and the confused and forlorn can get back some control in their lives. The message is crazy and absurd. The fact is, when you are dead, you will not be in control of your life, you will not be able to see out of the grave, and it won't matter to you whether your family mourns your death or not.

This ad sends a message that is quite the opposite of its intent. The same can be said of a billboard found in many major cities that is meant to warn children about the dangers of drugs. The billboard displays illegal drugs and drug paraphernalia under the headline: "Pushers Get Rich. Users Get Sick." What that billboard is saying is, "Be a pusher, you'll get rich. Be a user, you'll get sick." We get so wrapped up in trying to rationalize the practical side of an issue, we lose sight of the words we say and the messages we send.

With all our technological advancements in the information age, you might think that society would begin spreading some truths about death and dying. But this won't happen in a society that continues to refer to the comatose as "vegetables." Society would have us believe that by taking the comatose out of the realm of the human and putting them into the realm of the vegetative, we are making death more practical.

But there is a method behind society's madness that will allow us to continue to do what we have always done: harvest the dead. After all, if we see them as "vegetables," we can harvest them; or at least, we can harvest the vegetables' organs.

In a large metropolitan newspaper, the headline of a feature article on transplanting organs read, "Harvesting Organs." They didn't think you'd read the article with the uncatchy headline: "Harvesting Humans." That wouldn't be good business! Harvesting vegetables makes more sense, especially when you consider that people today don't die, they "expire," "perish," or generally just "go bad."

Death as a Mistake

Society would have us believe that death is weird, unbelievable, and in bad taste. When we don't buy that argument, society encourages us to make death practical. And when this doesn't fit with our need to deny the reality of death, we let ourselves believe that death is a mistake.

In response to Col. Blake's death in M*A*S*H, one viewer wrote that she planned to boycott the sponsor's product until the matter was "corrected." We may laugh at this, but it tells me that our unreal, untruthful concept of death, even for-entertainment-only death, is a serious problem.

I was recently eating lunch with a dear friend of mine when she asked if I had heard the terrible news. Well, there's so much terrible news being reported today, I had to ask, "What news was that?"

"Oh, the news of the sixteen-year-old boy who died at the medical center," my friend explained. "Why, the parents should sue that hospital." I asked why. My friend answered, "Well, if not the hospital, then they should at least sue those darned doctors."

I asked why the parents should sue anyone, and my friend replied, "Well, the boy went into the hospital yesterday complaining of abdominal pains, and died a few hours later of a ruptured appendix."

Again, I asked why the parents should sue the hospital or the doctors. My friend argued. "Come on, Dick, sixteen-year-old kids don't die of a ruptured appendix. Somebody must have made a mistake."

"Nope, no mistake. Kids of all ages die of ruptured appendixes. They do, and he did," was my response.

"Well, then he died before his time."

"Nope. It was his time to die, and he died."

Why would we think a death must mean someone made a mistake? Because a mistake can be erased. Malpractice suits are a kind of eraser for death in our society. Doctors and hospitals pay billions of dollars a year in malpractice insurance premiums because death is not supposed to happen. The emergency team didn't respond quickly enough, or the physicians weren't trained correctly, or the hospital didn't have the right equipment to deal with the injury or illness. Somebody screwed up somewhere because somebody is dead.

Death has to be a mistake. People aren't supposed to die, especially people we love. At least, not until they've reached a ripe old age, had what we suppose to be a full life, and most importantly, outlived us. Maybe we just don't want to face death because we are afraid of grief. Maybe we fear grief because we don't know how to work through it. Maybe if we knew how to work through our grief, we could accept the reality of death.

Death as Unreal

Certainly, grief can be painful; it is often accompanied by suffering. Maybe that's why we would rather not accept the fullness and reality of death. But I think it's simpler than that. I think we know that working through grief means accepting change in our lives, and we don't like change. The death of a loved one forces us to change, so death must be a mistake. If not a mistake, then death must be made practical. If not practical, then death must be weird, unbelievable, and in bad taste. If not, then there's only one thing left for us to do: deny death completely.

There are many ways to deny death. The most obvious is through the use of euphemisms—substituting pleasant, agreeable terms for unpleasant or disagreeable ones. People don't die in this day and age, they just seem to "go bad," right? When someone dies, he or she "croaked," "bought the farm," "deep six'd it," or "bit the dust." The newly dead have gone on to "pay the piper," "push up daisies," "give up the ghost" or "do the lawn-limbo."

A member of a Midwestern emergency medical team told me that they don't say D.O.A. (Dead On Arrival) anymore; it's too close to reality. They use a new term, T.T.A.D., or Toe Tagged At the Door. In the South I heard it was A.D.D.— All Done Dancing.

Once, while listening to a sermon at a funeral, I heard a description of death that was tough for me to swallow. The speaker said the deceased had "cut loose his moorings on the ship of life." I'm still not sure how the deceased actually died.

In big cities, people don't die. They expire, like parking meters. Expire, as in "date of expiration?" As in "he ran out of time, Jack?" What keeps us from saying "dead" and "died?" We treat them like four-letter words.

We especially have trouble saying "dead" or "died" to family members. Sometimes we think the words are just too much for the survivors to take. We don't want to do anything that might push them over the edge. Believe me, if survivors of death can't hear the words "dead" and "died," they won't hear much of anything else that is said to them.

Up North, people don't die. They "pass away" or "pass on." Down South, people just "pass." "You know old Billy Joe? He passed the other day."

Society even uses euphemisms to describe the place where we bury dead bodies. It used to be called a "necropolis," which means "city of the dead." When somebody sent you to work "out of the necropolis," you knew where you were headed. Today, you can't be so sure.

Society began to have some doubts about the bodies buried in the necropolis. Are they really dead? They could just be asleep, you know. Better that we call it a "cemetery," which is Latin for "resting or sleeping place."

Nowadays, the word "cemetery" might show up in horror novels, but we tend to refer to the cemetery as a "memorial park and garden." A park and garden, where people play and things grow.

Let your fingers do the walking through the Yellow Pages some day and you might find the Forest Park Cemetery. Sounds nice, doesn't it? Peaceful. A park in the woods. You could probably get a lot of rest there. Read down the ad and you'll see that Forest Park is "A Place for Perpetual Care" as well. Wow! You can go there as your final resting place and receive perpetual or continuous care. But when you're dead, are you really going to need perpetual care?

If that doesn't suit your fancy, keep looking. How about Pleasant View Memorial Park? Sounds like everybody has a good view in that place. Plus, it's a memorial park. Every day someone will commemorate your death. I don't know that that's something I'll care much about when I'm dead. Read on, and you learn that Pleasant View provides "pre-need planning." After all, it's in your best interests to plan for the burial of your dead body now before you are dead. That way you will have fewer worries when you die.

Trust me, when you are dead, you won't need the things these places provide. Whether your survivors will need them is something entirely different. But when you're dead, it won't be your problem, much less something you can do anything about.

The people we rely on most to provide clear, concise, and accurate information at the time of a death will also feed our denial. If you're ever in a funeral home and someone invites you "to the slumber room," believe me, you're in the wrong place. There is no body "sleeping" in that room. This is a child-like concept of death. When someone is dead, that person is not sleeping or resting.

Our denial of death goes beyond the use of euphemisms. From laypeople to professionals, from governments to institutions, we all play a role in denying death.

The Future of Death

As long as we continue to use inaccurate synonyms for a word we can't even define, we lead each other down a primrose path of untruth. But then, when you consider that some people suggest that no one has to die at all in this day and age, you get an accurate picture of where our society is headed.

Look at cryogenic preservation. Cryogenic preservation once referred to a method used to preserve lab samples. Now it is used to describe the process of preserving a dead body. The body is preserved in a "forever flask," instead of a casket.

Today, people who are cryogenically preserved are suspended in a forever flask as liquid nitrogen is vented in and around the body. At some date in the distant future, when relatives decide to thaw the body out, they are hoping there will be a cure for the cancer or heart disease or ailment which caused the person to die in the first place.

One woman had a window installed in her father's forever flask so she could come by on a regular basis to read to him from the daily newspaper. She believes that when her father is thawed out, he will be better able to cope because he'll have an updated impression of the state of the world.

Death as a Force in Our Lives

We are all experts on the subject of death and dying. We may hear that death is weird, unbelievable, and in bad taste. We may hear that death can be made practical, or it can be denied. One thing we know for certain is that death has tremendous power in our lives. But have you ever stopped to consider how that power is manifested?

Females being born today have a life expectancy of 83.2 years; for males, it's 76.4 years. Life expectancy statistics are frequently compiled by or for the benefit of insurance companies, which are motivated by profit. Still, the statistics are averages, and they are close enough to serve as a reference.

Many of you are married. Some of you have families. Do you have any idea why? Did your reason for marrying or having kids have anything to do with death? You are probably thinking that it had more to do with sex, but it is actually related to death and one's life expectancy. The thought of death forces us to act, to marry, and to have children, whether we're ready or not.

Can you imagine? Our fear of death forces us to have children. And all this time you thought it was sex, right? If we have children, we will never die. Children bring instant immortality; you will never die because you will live on through them. And it's likely that you'll spend a good part of your life hoping your children will have children, too.

Remember when your first child was born and you went to show off the kid to your family? You carried the little bundle into the room, and the whole family exclaimed, "Oh yes, it looks just like you!" Then your partner took the child to meet the other side of the family, and everybody exclaimed to your partner, "Oh yes, it looks just like you!" Both families felt they would live on through the child.

When my brother's second child was two days old, our mother saw the new baby and shouted, "Oh, it looks just like you, Bruce!" The poor kid was all wrapped up, head to toe, with this little blanket across his face, and my mother thought the child looked just like Bruce.

We have such a fear of death and dying that we even name our children "Junior" to keep ourselves alive. We name our kids after grandpas and grandmas. If you are one so named, you understand. Some people name their child after a saint. Saints never die.

But whether we like it or not, death is with us to the end. We can't avoid it, deny it, or redefine it. Death will be nothing more and nothing less than what it is: the end of physical life as we know it, on this physical earth as we understand it. We know we are not immortal, and mortality forces us to look at life from a very personal perspective.

Our understanding (or misunderstanding) of death forces us to marry. It forces us to have children. Death should force us to love, too, but when we start out with a misleading concept of death, it's no wonder we sometimes get things wrong.

Funeral processions should never take the quickest and easiest route to the cemetery. They should drive right through the middle of town, waving death in front of as many people as possible. Then that procession might motivate one person to call a loved one and say, "You know, dear, I really love you."

Or one person might go home that night and sit with his or her partner and ask "Who are we? What's going on with us? What's important in our lives? Why are we doing what we are doing?"

I like driving through towns where the cemetery is right out on the main road and everybody who drives by has to see it. Maybe when people in that town get to their destination, having driven right by the cemetery, they'll call up their spouse and say, "I love you." Just maybe. Maybe they will decide to get out of the crummy job they've hated for twenty years and change their lives for the better.

Death should force us to look at ourselves, to examine this thing we call life. Life is a highly desirable thing, but people often don't see it that way. They only see the pain and suffering, because along with an unreal, mistaken view of death goes an unreal, mistaken view of life.

We could help ourselves and each other know life. One way to do that is to quit supporting the denial of death. When we begin to appreciate the realities of death, we start to appreciate the joys of life—and share our newfound joys with others.

Death as Desirable

When you think about it, death is highly desirable. How many of us have taken fifteen minutes to think about what our lives would be like if we never died? Just think how important death is, how valuable and desirable it is. For most of us, the only time we think of death as desirable seems to be when there is suffering, old age, or a sense of uselessness.

The words "good-bye" mean, "God be with you." Today we say "have a nice day," instead. In some states we say, "don't forget your seat belt." I live in such a state, and my wife always tells me that if I died in a car accident and wasn't wearing my seat belt, she'd kill me.

Do you ever say good-bye? The other day, when you went off to work in the morning, did you say good-bye to your significant other? Did you actually say "good-bye," or something more like "See you tonight, honey?"

Why don't we say good-bye, as if it could be the end of a relationship? First, we don't like to end relationships. Even thinking about it is weird, unbelievable, and in bad taste. Second, we want to believe that we'll see our significant other later; we don't want to imagine anything different.

No, we don't end relationships well. We don't know how to. Maybe we're afraid we'll have to start them up all over again, even if it's only at the end of our workday. We need to say good-bye more often, and we need to mean it. Then we can begin to work on saying hello. If we work at ending our relationships, we can work at beginning them again.

As a marriage counselor, I see numerous relationship problems that arise when couples never say good-bye to each other. They come into my office and say, "Dick, we're thinking of getting a divorce. We don't talk anymore. We've both changed. This is not the same person I married. We've just grown apart."

I don't understand how people can "grow apart." They live together in the same house. They eat dinner together at the same table. They watch some of the same TV shows together every week. They have the same kids and sleep in the same bed. How in the world do they grow apart?

I think people grow apart when they don't say good-bye to each other every time they part company, even if it's only for a few hours. When they see each other again, they don't say hello and begin their relationship all over again.

You change each and every day. Tonight you will not be the same person you were this morning. You will have changed, maybe in a minuscule way. It's the same with your significant other. If you care about each other, and don't share with each other how you've both changed today, it won't be long before it seems you have grown apart.

Reading this book can wreck your relationship with your significant other. If the information in this book makes you respond to something differently than your spouse or partner expected, he or she will think, "Who is this person? We seem to be growing apart."

The next time you attend a social function, listen to how people describe the one you care about. You can tell a lot about your relationship if you find yourself thinking "Whoa! Has this person ever changed!"

If you are consistently working at reactivating, rebuilding, and replenishing your primary relationships, you are recognizing the fact that death hasn't happened to you today. You are a survivor. Today, you are among the living.

How many times have you heard a survivor mourn, "And I didn't even get to say good-bye!" This sounds the same as, "I never got to say I love you." If you don't end a relationship often and with sincerity, that relationship will always be hanging out there in some incomplete state. If you never say good-bye, you never really say hello. Death should force us to say hello, to once again get to know the people we love.

You may have heard estimates that 46% to 50% of all the people who get married today will be divorced within five years. There are plenty of theories to explain this statistic. Some people say that the divorce rate is high because people are less religious than in the past. Others suggest it has to do with social mobility: people are moving up and out so fast that they never develop a close network of supportive friends. Some say the divorce rate is high because more women are entering the work force. There are all kinds of theories, but I think we miss the most likely reason for divorce—death.

In an age where life expectancy has reached the seventies and eighties, people have many years to ask themselves, "How long will I be able to endure this bad relationship?" When the reality of death occurs to us, we realize that we may not get out of our relationships alive. It motivates some of us to take a closer look at our relationships, and some of that scrutiny results in divorce.

Death is not weird. Death is not unbelievable or in bad taste. Death will not be made practical. As much as we would like to deny it, death is real. It is a part of each and every life on this earth. The fact that each of us will die someday is big news to many people, and I don't understand why. Good news or bad, it's still a reality. The probability of death is one hundred percent. In one lifetime, each and every one of us will be dead. D-E-A-D dead—not "expired," not "passed on," not "gone bad"—dead.

But until we are dead, we are survivors. And as survivors, death can force us to love life and all that life has to offer. In that sense, death is highly desirable.

Chapter Two

THE THIRD WORLD
OF THE DYING

In the past, there were basically two worlds for writers, philosophers, and heroes to explore. One was the world of the living; the other, the world of the dead.

The world of the dead, for the most part, was to be found in necropolises—cities of the dead. Necropolises were often located on the outskirts of cities, because the living were afraid of catching what were often fatal diseases from dead bodies. The living kept this world of the dead away from water supplies, food markets, dwellings, and farms, away from anything that could be infected. When a person died, the dead body was ceremoniously carried into the world of the dead in a way that everyone could see. The holes for burial were dug just deep enough to bury the body, and a small cross or marker was placed on the grave. Anthropologists have coined the phrase "rite of incorporation" to signify this ceremonial ritual.

Throughout history, this rite of incorporation has also been known as "the funeral." This ritual still serves to move bodies from the world of the living to the world of the dead. But since the threat of catching diseases from dead bodies has diminished, both the funeral and the cemetery have taken on new meaning to the living.

You have to admit that the funeral is of little significance to the dead. If you believe that the dead are not actually dead and gone, but only "passed away," "expired," or gone to some "eternal resting place," then you may believe that they actually care about the color of their casket, the music played at their funeral, the sincerity, frequency, or degree of mourning exhibited by survivors, and the view from their hillside grave. But the real purpose of the ceremony is to answer the needs and fears of the living, not of the dead.

In the past, only two groups of people could traverse the worlds of the dead and the living: clergy and funeral directors. They are still thought to have one foot in the world of the living and one foot in the world of the dead.

Today, individuals need not be clergy or funeral directors to live in both worlds. Patients in hospitals, nursing homes, and hospice centers may also be traversing the worlds of the dead and the living. Some are brain dead, some have dead kidneys, some have dead lungs. Many are being kept alive with life-support equipment, which keeps their hearts pumping and their lungs breathing. These individuals inhabit the fringes of the world of the dead, yet they are being kept in the world of the living. They comprise the third world of the dying.

Because the elderly and the terminally ill still make up the largest percentage of the dying, and because they are cared for in hospitals, nursing homes, and hospice centers, the third world of the dying has grown to include the professionals who work at these facilities: critical-care nurses, hospice nurses, nursing home staff, doctors, clergy, funeral directors, and others.

These people are very much in the world of the living, yet they work with the dying on a daily basis. They witness death and grief every day. While many professionals appear to be mentally sound and spiritually alive, others seem dead to life—in part, because they have never come to terms with death. They have no concept of what is going on with the dying, the dead, or the survivors.

Today's graduating nurse may have never been to a funeral and is unlikely to have been around anyone near death. Many new nurses have never even seen a dead body, let alone touched one. Suddenly, they are told to prepare a body for the morgue. They don't know how to react to a dead body, and few people, even professionals, can offer any advice.

Nurses are the ones most often called upon to decide the DNR (Do Not Resuscitate) status of patients. They will say that doctors are the only ones who can make these decisions, but frankly, that's not true.

Whenever I speak to a group of nurses, I give them an assignment called "Who gets the heart?" I describe a scenario which includes four patients: a sixty-five-year-old man, a forty-five-year-old mother with a five-year-old child, a brilliant, thirty-three-year-old scientist, and a twenty-five-year-old registered nurse. Each of these patients desperately needs a donor heart to survive, but there is only one heart available. Who gets the heart?

The nurses invariably say they don't like "playing God," and most don't want to participate in the exercise. They don't realize that they do the same thing all the time on the job. When a doctor needs to be called in to an emergency, the nurses are frequently the ones who determine the code of the call.

"No, Dick," the nurses say. "The doctor puts that order on a patient's chart, in case the need to resuscitate arises."

"Wait a minute. How much of the time is the doctor actually there with the patient in such an emergency?"

"Not often."

"Then you are the ones who have to decide if you are going to carry out whatever orders the doctor has written. You decide the code. You decide the DNR status. You make the final decision." The nurses have to agree.

Doctors often tell me that they don't understand why nurses get so upset on the job. It is the doctors, they claim, who make the life and death decisions. But when I explain that nurses are the ones most often called upon to make these decisions, doctors admit that they've never given it much thought.

It is amazing how such separation and distance can be found among staff who work so closely with one another. These people deal with life and death, yet they are often unaware of each other's perception of reality. And for some, that perception is grossly distorted.

You might imagine that critical-care nurses have a clear understanding of what it means for a person to be dead, especially when they are following a doctor's orders. Research shows that when nurses remove the tubes, wires, and monitors from a patient who had been on life-support, 80% of those nurses will pull the bed rails up on the dead patient's bed. Why? Because most nurses apparently believe the dead patient is only a little bit dead, not D-E-A-D dead. That's the same as believing someone is just a little bit pregnant.

I was recently in a morgue in a large Midwestern community when I ran across an advertisement posted on an employee bulletin board. The ad promoted the "cct-100," or concealed cadaver transporter. I have no idea how many concealed cadaver transporters the manufacturer has sold, but I imagine quite a few.

The concealed cadaver transporter is a special gurney designed to transport dead bodies. The gurney has a false top that conceals a lower compartment, which is covered with a sheet. The gurney is wheeled into the room of a patient who has died, and the sheet is removed. The body is placed on the gurney and the sheet is replaced over the false top. The gurney containing the body can then be wheeled down the hall with no one suspecting that anyone has died.

If an institution doesn't happen to have a cct-100, they have what I call the "door guard." It's all part of an institution's "closed door policy." When a patient dies, a funeral director or staff member from the morgue is called to come and remove the body from the patient's room. When this person arrives, the nurses run down the hallway and close the doors to the other patients' rooms. From the end of the hallway, one nurse gives the "all clear" signal. The funeral director or staff member wheels the body from the room and steals away to the facility's hidden morgue or loading dock.

This is a good example of "team medicine." I've seen almost everybody get into the act. I have seen administrators play the role of hall guard. I have seen clergy shut the doors to patients' rooms. I have seen doctors and even volunteers give the "all clear" signal. But no matter who's involved in the game, when the doors are reopened, the patients almost always ask, "Who died?"

Whenever I see them play this game, I ask the staff what they are trying to accomplish. I've heard all the answers. Most often I'm told that "hospital or facility policy prevents visitors from seeing dead bodies" because "it's bad PR."

A few years ago a hospital brought a lawsuit against a major daily newspaper, preventing the paper from stating the name of that hospital in obituaries. The hospital happened to be one of the best emergency-care facilities in the state, so it received an exceptionally high number of patients in critical condition. Consequently, a large number died from their injuries, and the hospital became known not as the best critical-care facility in the state, but as "the Hospital of Death."

Medical facilities want to protect patients and visitors from exposure to death and dying. This might be practical, from an economic standpoint. But I believe the closed-door policies at hospitals have more to do with the desire to protect hospital staff than with economics.

Most hospital administrators are aware that nurses and doctors are caring, compassionate people. They wouldn't be in the profession if they weren't. They are also human. They build relationships with some, if not all, of the patients they care for. Staff members often are emotionally invested in their patients. The patients become extended family, in a sense. This is especially true in critical-care facilities. Patients with terminal illnesses are kept alive longer than ever before, and staff become emotionally involved with the struggles of these patients. When they die—and terminal-illness patients do die—the staff feel grief.

The advertisement for the cct-100 describes the product as a hidden solution to a difficult problem. From all outward appearances, an empty stretcher is being wheeled down the hallway, eliminating distasteful experiences for others (i.e., staff). The closed-door policies in facilities are designed to accomplish the same thing: the elimination of distasteful experiences for staff— the lumps in the throats, the tears in the eyes, the aches in the hearts of the nurses, doctors, clergy, and volunteers who have grown to know and love the patients who die. But believe me, these emotions will still be there, regardless of the cct-100 or the shutting of doors. You can't shut off the grief that follows death.

Those Who Work with the Dying

Many of you reading this book are professionals—doctors, oncology nurses, funeral directors, hospice volunteers, or members of the clergy. You are experts on the third world of the dying. You already know how society sees you and your relationship with the dead or the terminally ill.

Let's say that you are a hospice nurse. All day long you provide emotional and physical care for the terminally ill. One day you go to your class reunion, where you see friends you haven't seen since high school. These friends knew you were studying to become a registered nurse. They admired you and your humanitarian goals, but they had no real sense of what you would do for a living.

At the Turn Back the Clock Dance and Reception, you find yourself reminiscing with a couple of old friends. One asks, "Weren't you studying to be a nurse?"

"Yes, and college was grand! That's where I met Bill, my husband," you reply.

"Oh, you're married? And you probably have a dozen kids of your own," your friends laugh. "So, are you working as a nurse now?"

You say, "Yes, I'm a shift supervisor at St. Someone-Or-Other's."

"Oh, that's nice! Isn't that just the nicest . . . wait a minute," they query, "isn't that The Nationally Famous Medical Center down south?"

"Why, yes!"

They grin with restraint. "Well, isn't that a hospital for children who are all dying of cancer?"

"Yes? . . ."

Now, correct me if I'm wrong, but don't people often respond with something like, "Yuck, I'd hate that job! I couldn't imagine taking care of those kids. How can you do that?"

If you say, "I work in a nursing home," the response is often, "Yuck! How can you do that?"

If you say, "I work with people who are dying with AIDS," the response is probably, "Yuck! How can you do that?"

If you say, "I'm a funeral director," the response will most certainly be, "Yuck! How can you do that?"

If you tell your friends that you've been doing a lot of reading lately, and one of the best books you've come across is about surviving death and grief, "Yuck! How can you read something like that?" is the likely response.

The comments, the questioning looks, and the I-could-never-do-that's are another way of saying, "weird, unbelievable, and in bad taste." Funeral directors call this response the "hidden-hand syndrome." If you've just made friends with a funeral director—which is unlikely, unless you are one yourself—introduce your new friend to others at a social function. They will stick out their hand in greeting and ask, "What is it you do for a living?" When told, they will quickly put their hands behind their back as if they were just about to touch something weird, unbelievable, and in bad taste. Then they will quietly disappear to the other side of the room.

Ask yourself if you would get on an elevator with a funeral director to go to the thirteenth floor. "Yuck! No way. Don't want to get too close to that person!"

A lot of important research has been done on elevators, some quite remarkable. Imagine a pathologist coming to work in the morning in standard business clothes. No one would think twice about getting on an elevator with that person. Put the same person in a smock, and fewer will go along for the ride. Give the doctor a clipboard and an official name tag that says pathologist, and hardly anyone will take the elevator. Smock, clipboard, name tag and gurney with a covered body? Forget it! It's a lonely ride on the elevator for that doctor. The more "death-related" the person appears, the less others are willing to relate to him or her.

If you ask a member of the clergy to dinner one evening, and the invitation is declined because the person has to officiate at a funeral, what do you think? If he or she promises to come over right after the funeral, won't you be just a little bit sorry you invited him or her over in the first place?

"You'd never catch me doing *that* for a living!" That's the weird part. "How could anyone do that job?" That's the unbelievable part. "You brought *who* to the party?" That's the in-bad-taste part.

To have a true understanding of death and grief, it is important that we understand our perception of death and dying. If we believe that death is weird, unbelievable, and in bad taste, this is how we will perceive people who are dying or grieving. We will be unable to provide the care and support that the dying and the grieving need most.

The Care We Give

Much of my work involves listening and talking to people who work and live in the third world of the dying. I have visited with professionals and hospice patients across the country. I have counseled clergy, nurses, and friends and family members of the dead. I am often told how we professionals fall short in the care we provide to the grieving.

Because we have our own fears of dying and grieving, we find it difficult to distinguish between our own needs and the needs of others. My work has led me to assemble a list of needs that I believe many hospice patients have. While writing this list, I tried to put myself in the hospice patient's shoes. It has helped me (as well as others, I hope) to see things outside of myself, from the eyes of one who needs care and support.

Hope

As a hospice patient, I would want hope. I would want a whole lot of hope. Real, honest, and sincere hope—not false, patronizing hope. As I am faced with my own mortality, hope is the only thing I know that is eternal. Hope may change, but, at the same time, hope is infinite.

Some years ago, a friend of mine had problems with his throat. He went to a physician, explained that his throat was sore all the time, and asked for help. He told the doctor, "I hope it's nothing serious." After the examination, the doctor suggested that my friend visit a specialist to have a biopsy taken. My friend said, "I hope it's not too bad." After the biopsy, the specialist told my friend he had a malignant tumor on his vocal cords and then scheduled surgery. My friend commented, "I hope the doctors can get all of the tumor."

After the operation, the doctor told my friend they could not remove all of the tumor, and more surgery would be necessary. My friend said, "Wow! I hope I don't lose my voice." Over the next few weeks, my friend's voice began to fade. With what little voice he had left, my friend said, "I hope this won't grow to be too painful." As the pain increased, my friend was reduced to writing on a scratch pad to communicate with others. One of the first things he wrote was, "I hope this thing doesn't kill me." As the cancer spread through his body, the doctors told him he had little chance of survival. He wrote, "I hope I don't die this year."

As his strength diminished, my friend worked hard to accomplish what few things he could still do for himself. He began writing fewer messages and developed a kind of sign language to communicate with those who stayed close to him. I remember the gesture he acted out most often: he would wrinkle his eyebrows, smile as best he could, and raise his clenched fist to his chest. That was his sign for hope.

As my friend lay in his hospital bed, he hoped people wouldn't leave him to die alone. As the frequency of his visitors dropped, my friend hoped that he could die with dignity. When he became confined to his bed, he hoped he was "right" with his God. I sat at my friend's side and watched as his strength diminished and his hope for a miracle faded. He would look up at me with a feeble smile and squeeze my hand as hard as he could, a sign that he hoped I would not leave his side.

Each and every day, my friend hoped that he could fully live what life he had left. And to the end, my friend's hope never died. His hope changed, but it was with him to the very end of his life.

As a hospice patient, I don't want to hear anyone say, "There is no hope." I will hope until the end. And I want others to hope with me, to encourage my hope—even if that hope is, "I hope I can die soon."

Humor

As a hospice patient, I would want humor. We all use humor to ease the tension in serious situations. Humor is an important tool that helps us cope. If I had terminal cancer, I wouldn't want others to stop laughing with me. I would want them to joke with me, to tell me funny stories, to talk with me about the crazy things that are happening in their lives.

A lot of funny things happen in hospitals. I would want the nurses and doctors to share that humor with me. Funny things happen in churches. I would want the clergy to share that humor with me. As the time of my death grew closer, I would even want funeral directors to share their humor with me.

Without humor, the seriousness of my fateful situation would overwhelm me. And if you can't bring yourself to laugh with me, then at least bring me a book of jokes. Bring me calendars that have a new joke for every day of the week. If I read ahead a few months (because I don't know how long I'll live), laugh at those jokes with me, too. Get me a VCR, show me funny movies, and laugh with me. Buy me funny get-well cards, and, if I can't read them for myself, read them to me and laugh about them with me.

Help

If I were a hospice patient, I would want help, a lot of help. I would want you to help me die. Dying would be new to me, something I'd never done before. I would have no idea if I were doing it correctly. I would want you to help me with my family. I would want more than just an offer of emotional support to my grieving survivors, I would want to know that you would help teach my family the things I can't after I'm dead.

Home

As a hospice patient, I would want to be home, if possible. A large part of my life revolved around my home. I spent a lot of money providing that home for myself and my family. I've had some very good times in that home. Home is a special place to me. I helped design it and worked hard to make it what it is.

I understand there may come a time when I can't be at my home. But I would still have that hope. And if that hope changes, I would like to make my room in the hospice or nursing home feel as close to my home as possible.

Order

If I were a hospice patient, I would want some order in what life I had left. I would like to know what to expect, on a daily, even hourly, basis. At this enormously disorganized time in my life, I would want organization all around me. I would want the phone to be in the same place next to my bed every time I need to use it. I would want my toothbrush and comb where I could reach them, and cards and letters close so I could read them. If I have order around me, I can have some sense of security in the midst of my insecurity.

Openness

If I were a hospice patient, I would want openness. I would need people to be honest and open with me. I would want staff, family, and friends to tell me what's going on with them. If I have your complete and sincere openness, I will trust you. If you are closed and withdrawn, I will doubt you. I would want to trust that the entire staff—doctors, nurses, and volunteers—have my best interests at heart. I will trust that, if I see openness.

Options

As a hospice patient, I would also want options. I would want the option not to be awakened at 5 A.M. to be told that breakfast will come at 7 A.M. (I can't believe this has to be mandatory). I would want the option to sleep until noon, if I cared to. I would want the option to have my family sitting on the edge of my bed twenty-four hours a day, if that's what we need. Don't limit visiting hours, give me some options. I hope I would at least have the option to make some choices in what's left of my life.

Safety

As a hospice patient, I would want to feel safe. I've never died before. I would like to have other people around me going through the same thing, so I could check to see if the emotions I feel are normal. Fellowship would help me feel safe amidst all the mixed-up feelings that would certainly be going on inside me.

Sex

Yes, even as a hospice patient, I would need sex. This doesn't necessarily mean two hours of passionate love-making. It's much more simple than that. I will need someone to touch me, to hold me, to gently squeeze my hand. I will want some tender affection, some intimacy, and maybe some romance.

I may need some time alone with my intimate partner. That doesn't necessarily mean I would need sexual intercourse. It could mean closeness and cuddling and touching and laying together. Don't get the crazy notion that my need for sex means a need for intercourse. You may remember a time when holding hands was quite sexual. Well, let me be sexual.

Sharing

If I were a hospice patient, I would want you to share a part of yourself with me. Sharing is important, because if you know me intimately, I need to know you the same way. You will come to know my private hurts and pains. You will come to learn some of my best-kept secrets. And you will find out some of my darkest fears. I need to know that you are willing to share some of the same parts of yourself. If you can't share things with me, I will want to know why. If you are afraid to share because investing in a relationship with me means you will have to grieve my death, I will share some things that will help you deal with your grief.

Sadness

As a hospice patient, I want you to be sad. I want you to be really sad, too. During my pain, I will want you to cry. As I'm dying, I will want you to cry. I will want you to tell me you'll miss me after I die. I will want to know that after I'm dead and gone, you will mourn the loss of your friend. Your sadness will make me feel special.

Spirituality

If I were a hospice patient, spiritual things would be very important to me. That doesn't necessarily mean I will need a lot of religious support. That doesn't mean you have to send the chaplain to read to me from the Bible every day. It does mean I will want to talk with you about your philosophies and opinions. I will want to talk to you about life and death and mortality and eternity. To some, spirituality is music that plays in the background of their entire lives. I would like to dance to the sound of that symphony, until the very end.

Freedom from Pain

If I were a hospice patient, I would want to be pain-free. I don't think that's a lot to ask. I'd like to be aware of things going on around me but stay as pain-free as possible. I will try to remember that I need to experience some pain if I'm going to remain sensitive to others around me. But in my fatal illness, I will have plenty of emotional pain. And it may be that some physical pain can't be prevented. But I will want pain medication on a predictable, orderly basis. I won't want to have to ask every time I need relief from pain.

Privacy

As a hospice patient, I may need privacy at times. I might need privacy for an entire two or three days. Just because I need privacy doesn't mean I'm depressed, it means I need to be alone.

We've all felt the need to be alone. If you were to come home from work one day to find your family standing in front of your home that just burned to the ground, you would need some support. You would want people to care, to hug, and to cry with you. But there would come a time when you'd say, "I just need to be alone for a while. I need to sort out all of these feelings I have, and find out who I am now, after this loss."

When I tell you I need privacy, just shut the door to my room. It doesn't mean I'm going crazy. When I need you again, I'll let you know. That's what that little buzzer next to my bed is for. At times I will need privacy with my God, privacy with members of my family, maybe even privacy with you. Please be able to give me what I need.

Individuality

Even as a hospice patient, I will want to be an individual with my own identity. I won't want to be just another terminally-ill patient in a hospital full of dying people. I won't want to feel like just another statistic that will live on in some doctor's research paper. I will want to be an individual, the unique human being that I am. I will want to be me for as long as I can.

Insecurity

If I were a hospice patient, I would feel insecure at times. I might be afraid of the doctors, and you will probably want to make me feel secure. I might be afraid of some forms of treatment, and you will want to give me some sense of security. I will be afraid of dying, and you will try to give me the security of your life. In my illness, your false security won't help me much, so at times, just let me be insecure.

Interests

As a hospice patient, I would still like to have my own interests. Today, I'm interested in the variety and excitement life has to offer. If I were dying, my interests may not be as important to me, but that will be my choice. I don't want you to tell me I can't pursue my interests.

I am interested in photography. If you see me taking pictures in your hospital, I would like you to help me work out any issues that might arise concerning other patients' rights to privacy. I would like you to help me get my photos developed, and maybe you could help me frame one or two of my pictures to hang in my room. Don't make it difficult for me to pursue my interests.

Independence

As a hospice patient, I would like to feel independent for as long as possible. I know that sooner or later I won't be able to do some things for myself. At some point in my illness, I may grow more and more dependent on others. Even if I become dependent upon you, I would like you to give me some independence. If the time comes for me to get an injection, let me pick which side of my bottom I get that injection in. It may seem like a small thing to ask, but it will give me a sense that I still have some control over what is left of my life. That may be all the control I can handle, but at least I would be sure I'm still alive.

Communication

If I were a hospice patient, I would want as much communication as possible. If there are tubes and wires running in and around me, get me whatever I need to communicate. It may not seem to you that I'd have much of anything important to say, but I guarantee that what I have to say will mean the world to me.

Contact

As a hospice patient, I will want to maintain contact with the outside world. I will want to know what the real temperature is outside, and about the only way I would be able to get that information is by keeping in contact through you. If I ask, and you tell me it's hot outside, I will want to know how hot. I'll want you to tell me if it's sweaty hot or dry hot or cool hot. Even if the outside world is just down the hall at the nurses' station, I'll want you to take the time to keep me in contact with that world.

I will want a television, and probably a VCR. When my family sends me a videotape of my child's graduation, I'll want to watch it on my TV. It would be nice if you made me a videotape of your neighborhood cookout or softball game or carnival, or whatever is of interest to you.

And please, don't tell me that it can't be done. I know a little bit about this information age. I know that every hospital has a VCR and a camcorder. I know it's not that difficult to make a twenty-minute videotape of what's going on in the park down the street. I know what life is, and I'll want to keep in contact with life until the last possible moment.

Excitement

As a hospice patient, I would also want a little excitement. I love to hear what other people are up to. I know that hospital staff sometimes manipulate their administrations. Those stories are fun and exciting to me, and I want to hear them all. I want to hear about who's having an affair with whom. I want to know how you feel about your shift leader. I want to hear about the place you go to worship. I want to hear about your children. And I promise, I won't share your deepest secrets with anyone. I would have nothing to gain if I did. I just don't want to stop feeling excitement.

Experiences

If I were a hospice patient, I wouldn't want to stop having experiences. When a person is dying, it seems that everyone around that person wants to talk in the past. "Do you remember the day . . ." "Boy, I'll never forget the time . . ." "I'll never forget, you laughed so hard . . ."

All that talk about the past is for the survivors. And my survivors will need to talk as they work through their grief after I die. But if I'm not dead yet, please don't dwell in the past. Give me some new experiences every day. Teach me games I've never played before. Read to me from a book I've never heard of. Show me pictures of places I've never seen. I want to know about new things. And if you've heard of new, experimental drugs being used for other patients who have my same illness, I'd be interested in trying them out. Keep the newness and freshness of life alive for me through experiences.

These are some of the things that I imagine I would want if I were a hospice patient. To me, very much alive and well, they don't seem like too much to ask for. To you, if you were caring for me through my terminal illness, it might be tough. It might be tough for you to give so much of yourself, especially if you are in the midst of grieving. But I work with loss and grief everyday, and I know that as you work to provide care for me, you are actually helping yourself. When you give of yourself in the interest of others, even in the midst of your grief, you are able to come to terms with the fullness and reality of what you have now, before it is lost. And that work will make your grief easier to process.

Trust me.

Chapter Three

THE BEREAVED

Before we take a closer look at how society views grief and the grieving, I'd like to define three key terms we use when talking about death or loss: bereavement, grief, and mourning. Sometimes we use these terms interchangeable. By doing so, however, we fuel the fire of misconception, inhibiting the personal growth process that can, and should, take place in the midst of loss.

Bereavement, Grief, and Mourning

Bereavement, grief, and mourning are three distinct and separate human conditions. Bereavement is the state of being deprived. Grief is the emotion we feel as a result of being bereaved. Mourning is the expression of our grief and other feelings that come from being bereaved. Sometimes we apply these terms, especially grief and mourning, only to death. But each and every time we are deprived of something, we are bereaved. We will grieve, and we will express those feelings, whether we mean to or not, through mourning.

If you've made plans to have lunch with a friend and he or she calls to cancel or postpone your meeting, you are bereaved (deprived). You may feel offended (grief). When you eat an entire pan of brownies by yourself, that's mourning.

If you go home expecting your spouse and children to welcome you with open arms, but instead you find an empty home, you will be bereaved. You may feel lonely or rejected—that's grief. If you go to the liquor cabinet and pour yourself a Scotch, that's mourning.

If you turn on the TV to watch your favorite prime-time drama, and the program is preempted by a special address from the President, you will be bereaved (and probably peeved, too). The anger you feel at being deprived is grief. How you display that anger is mourning.

If you get angry when you happen to come upon a traffic detour, you are grieving. If you then drive that detour at 20 mph over the speed limit because you are angry, you are mourning. And when the police officer pulls you over to issue you a citation, and you suggest that you weren't really speeding, just "naturally processing your grief through mourning," you are suffering delusions!

In the morning, when your alarm clock wakes you up from a restful sleep, you will be bereaved. If you forget where you put your car keys, if your child goes off to college, or if you lose your job, you will be bereaved.

In each case, you will grieve and you will mourn. The intensity of your grief and mourning will depend on how much of yourself you had invested in what you lost.

Even if you experience a gain, you will feel some grief. It is a myth that positive events bring only happiness, delight, and joy. If you won the multimillion-dollar mega-bucks-bingo-lottery, all of your friends would expect you to be overjoyed. No more worries for you. You'd have financial security for the rest of your life. You could buy a new house, new car, new lifestyle. Winning the lottery would be a big gain for you.

But it could also be a big loss. You would lose your privacy. You might lose some old friends. At the least, you would lose the security of knowing who your real friends are. If you moved out of your old bungalow into a new estate, you would lose your home. You might lose your present job, your car, your clothes, your kids, your way of life. You could lose everything you have right now. Instead of feeling elated, you might need some intense grief counseling. (If so, be sure to call my office. I make special, long-term arrangements for lotto winners!)

The belief that loss means only pain, and gain means only happiness, is a myth. It only perpetuates the unfounded fears that keep us from accepting the reality of life. But we already know this, because we are all experts on loss and grief.

Experts on Loss and Grief

Each of us has gained invaluable knowledge through our personal experiences with loss and grief. We are experts.

If you are a New York Yankees fan, you're an expert on loss and grief. If you've ever been married, whether or not you've been divorced, you're an expert on loss and grief. If you've moved, changed jobs, lost your wallet, or had children, then you are an expert on loss and grief.

Think of the things you can lose when you marry. Your freedom. Your money—at least, the choice to spend your money as you could before you were married. Your privacy, your last name, your virginity.

The point is, when you get married, you lose your identity—the person you were before you were married—and this is quite a loss. We only seem to see the gain that marriage has to offer, and we expect everyone involved to celebrate our happy circumstances.

If you are married, you probably recall standing at the front of a church or synagogue, with most of your friends and relatives present. Perhaps a group of complete strangers (the other side of the family, on the other side of the aisle) were there, too, and in the background, you heard your Aunt Sue crying.

As you stood in the receiving line, Aunt Sue walked up, tears still streaming down her face, and offered you a hug. Immediately you consoled her, "Oh, don't cry!" And she responded, "Happy tears! Yes, these are just happy tears. I'm so happy for you, I could just . . ." Sob-sob-sob.

Happy tears? You married some clown from Embarrass, Minnesota, and your aunt was crying happy tears?

Chances are, you and your aunt had been close. Now she would only see you at holidays and reunions. Your aunt felt a tremendous loss. Yet your response to this grief was likely, "Now, don't cry, Aunt Sue. You're not losing a niece, you're gaining a nephew!"

Parents, too, are experts on loss and grief. They know what you lose when you gain a child. Sleep, for one. The freedom to come and go as you please (at least for a while). Your relationship with your partner. My wife pointed this out four or five days after she brought our first child home from the hospital. She asked, "Why is it, Dick, that when you come home now, you kiss the baby first and not me?"

That gave me something to think about.

When you have children, you are apt to lose your privacy. Ever have a three-year-old child open up the bathroom door and yell, "Hi, Dad!"? It only happens at the most inconvenient time. And only if the bathroom is next to the family room, and it just so happens that you're entertaining your new neighbors that night.

When we have a children, we lose and lose and lose. Yes, we gain and gain and gain, too. But if we imagine that having children will mean *only* gain, who are we kidding? We know better. We know that when we gain a child, we are in for some big losses. We simply don't acknowledge it.

It begins in the hospital with the brand new parent standing in front of the "wonder window." A nurse walks up. The parent points to the little bundle of joy closest to the window and smiles. Does the nurse say, "You have my deepest sympathy?" Of course not.

Women remember what happens a couple of days, weeks, or months after childbirth. The tears start to well up inside, and the new mother just can't stop crying. Her husband comes home, sees the tears, and says, "But dear, you should be so happy!"

So the mother tries to straighten herself up. She tries to control the pain and stop the tears. The next time she visits the gynecologist, she tells her about all these "feelings."

All too often, her doctor says, "postpartum depression." But this may not be true. Depression is a serious mental illness. Here is a new mother just beginning to realize all the losses she has incurred, and all those she can look forward to. She is just beginning to understand the drastic changes that are happening in her life—and the doctor wants to treat her for depression. All this woman is doing is asking herself, "Who am I now?" This is what grief is all about: redefining yourself after you experience a loss.

If you graduated from high school, you are an expert on loss and grief. In a way, the graduation ceremony is a big funeral service to ritualize a big loss.

Think about it. Family and friends gather together. All of the graduates wear a cap and gown—quite solemn clothing. The music is a slow-paced, somber march—a requiem. After everyone is seated, some dignitary walks up to the front of the room and delivers a sermon. They call it the "commencement address," but it is really a solemn sermon in observance of the grand finale of high school. They just misnamed it.

The one word used most often in high school commencement addresses is the same word used most often in funeral services: *hope*. "We hope you enjoyed your four years here at Tinker-Toy Tech. We hope you go on to make your family and friends proud. We hope you enjoy success in your chosen career. We hope the rest of your life is filled with wonder and joy."

The ceremony ends with the recessional—another solemn march. Then there is a receiving line, and family and friends wait in front of the gymnasium to take pictures. You see receiving lines and friends gathering at funerals, too.

At some point, handshakes, hugs, and gifts are exchanged. If your high school graduation was anything like mine, many of the graduates went out and drank to medicate their grief.

At graduation, every child loses. They lose the teachers, friends, and enemies they had for the past four years, all in one big ceremony. They lose what had become a way of life.

My dad, like many dads in those days, had a rule: when you graduated, you moved out of the house. You had to get out in the world, get a job, get a place of your own. Back then, many of us graduates lost our homes. We lost our parents, too. I wonder where people get the idea that graduation (or marriage, or childbirth, or any other gain in life) doesn't include loss?

If you wear glasses, you're an expert on loss and grief. I received my first pair of glasses soon after I joined the military. The first three or four days of life in the armed services were tough for everybody. I found myself in a strange place, with strange people, doing some pretty strange things. And for three or four days, I got little or no sleep. At the end of those first days, the sergeant took all the new recruits in for a medical exam. The exam included an eye test.

Afterwards, I was called up to the front of the line, and an eye doctor bellowed, "Okay, Obershaw, here's your prescription for glasses. Next!"

I stopped in my tracks, turned to the doctor, and said, "Whoa, wait a minute! Wait just a minute! I don't think I need glasses, sir!"

He said, "Oh, yeah? Why's that?"

"Well," I explained, "The reason I can't see your blasted chart way back there is because I haven't had any sleep for three days and three nights."

He curtly replied, "How is it, soldier, you didn't get sleep only in your left eye?"

He had me there! I didn't know what to say. I needed glasses. I had lost part of my 20/20 vision, if only in one eye. This was a tremendous physical loss, and I grieved.

If you have had physical loss in your life—a mastectomy, a hysterectomy, a vasectomy—you know about loss and grief. You are an expert on the subject.

If you've had to relocate because of work, you've experienced loss. Not too long ago, a woman came into my office contemplating a divorce. When I asked her why, she said that her husband worked for a major corporation. He was required by his job to relocate often. "I've had to move eleven times in seven years! I will not move again. I want a divorce!"

This woman had experienced major losses in her life because of her husband's job. Every time she got settled in a new community, her husband got promoted and they moved again. She lost her home, friends, and security over and over again. These were major losses, and the result was major grief.

If we don't learn to recognize the losses in our lives, to identify the feelings that result from those losses, and to work through our grief, it isn't long before our grief overwhelms us. When we are overwhelmed, we want out. We want the sadness and hurt to stop, and we will do whatever it takes to stop the pain.

You may be an expert on loss and grief because you have experienced divorce. Ten years ago I was asked to speak to a church group about the grief that results from divorce. The church officials invited me under the condition that I not use the word "divorce." Instead, I spoke about the "death of a dream."

After years of working in marriage counseling and grief counseling, I have come to believe that the grief resulting from divorce is often more difficult to resolve than the grief resulting from death. There are a number of reasons why I believe this is true.

First, there are no funerals for "dead" marriages. There is no "rite of incorporation" for the person who used to live in the world of the married, but now must live in the world of the single.

Second, the relationship with an ex-spouse often doesn't end, even after the divorce. When a spouse dies, there is some closure to the relationship. But in divorce, you could always run into your ex at the shopping mall on vacation, or when one of you picks up the kids for the weekend.

Third, until recently, there were few support groups for survivors of dead marriages. Today, more and more divorce groups are there to help the divorced. But many of these groups can't provide the care and support that is necessary, because they are not prepared to help members work through their grief.

I like the idea of support groups for the newly divorced. Groups like these can help individuals come to terms with the loss of their dream. Tremendous support and care can be offered in a group setting. Furthermore, a strong bond tends to develop between individuals who experience a similar loss. Maybe divorce groups will someday ritualize the death of a marriage the way that physical death is ritualized.

Recently, a friend of mine who was in the process of getting a divorce heard me suggest the idea of a ritual to signify the end of a marriage. He thought it sounded like a good idea, so he scheduled a funeral for his marriage. He imagined it would be quite a party—a wake of sorts.

He invited all his friends, his former wife, and some of her friends. He scheduled the wake for the day after the divorce was final.

That day, we all gathered at this man's former home. He set up a Super-8 film projector and showed a movie of their wedding—in reverse. A car backed up to the church. He and his wife backed out of the car and walked backwards into the church. All of the rice went back into the hands of the guests. Back and back and back the film went.

The film was meant to bring some humor to a serious situation. When the movie began, there were laughs and chuckles in the room. But as it went on, the room grew more and more quiet.

Finally, the film came to the beginning—the bride walked down the aisle backwards and out of the church into the sunlight—and the reality of the divorce hit us all like a bombshell. The film was like an open casket at a funeral; there was much sadness in the room.

There were tears, hugs, and good-byes. It was not at all what my friend had expected, but it ended up being a healthy experience for us all. Most of the couples at the wake have maintained relationships with both my friend and his wife, which is not typical when a divorce occurs. Furthermore, there were fewer games, hurt feelings, and "hidden agendas" between the divorced couple.

We all got to say good-bye to the couple we had known for so long, and the couple got to say good-bye to the way they used to relate to each other. Everyone had an opportunity to come to terms with the emotions that resulted from the divorce.

We are all experts on loss and grief because we have all had points of bereavement in our lives. We have all mourned. Often, our mourning was considered by others—and perhaps by ourselves—as weird, unbelievable, and in bad taste.

Survivors are frequently denied the opportunity to experience the fullness of their loss. Because of our misconceptions surrounding loss and grief, we try to protect survivors from what we imagine to be unnecessary suffering. But our misguided desire to protect and support does more harm than good.

When pregnancy results in a stillborn baby, for example, the desire to protect the mother from "unnecessary grief" can ruin a marriage. When a baby is born dead, the first thing many hospitals do is move the mother from the obstetrics ward down to the general ward. They say that the crying babies in the obstetrics ward would only make the mother sad (as if the mother isn't sad already).

Then the doctors, nurses, clergy, and funeral directors approach the father with open arms. They help him arrange the funeral service, notify immediate family members, and prepare the baby's body for burial. During all of this, the mother is left back at the hospital.

The father has the opportunity to experience the fullness of the couple's loss. He can better process his grief because he has the support of the doctors, nurses, clergy, funeral directors, and family. Meanwhile, the mother lies in her hospital bed with empty arms, a rose from her baby's casket next to her bed.

To make matters worse, someone inevitably tells her, "Now, dear. Don't cry. Just be glad you're okay. You can always have another child."

When the mother comes home from the hospital, she will "search" for her stillborn child. She will probably live a good part of her life never having processed her grief—in part, because we've taken it upon ourselves to deny her the opportunity to experience the fullness of her loss. We imagine that the mother is emotionally or physically incapable of handling the reality of the loss, so we do our best to hide that loss from her.

Hospital staff generally agree that mothers don't process their grief over a stillbirth as completely as fathers. But they say it's because mothers are different. "Mother's have a different bond with their babies. Fathers process their grief better because they aren't as attached." I strongly disagree. Fathers are better able to process their grief because they are given a chance to experience the fullness of the couple's loss.

Have you ever wondered why hospital staff sometimes discourage mothers from seeing and holding the body of their stillborn baby? Because they feel it is weird, unbelievable, and in bad taste. I've actually been told that mothers don't need to see the body of a stillborn, because mothers already know what babies look like.

When a baby is stillborn, the mother is whisked away from all the other mothers and told not to worry, she can always have another child. As she lays there alone, she thinks, "If they won't even let me see my baby, or touch my baby, or love my baby, it must look horrible!"

A mother denied the opportunity to see, hold, and say good-bye to her stillborn baby may live the rest of her life with terrible illusions about the baby and the stillbirth. She will have been denied the fullness of her loss, as well as the fullness of the care and support she might have otherwise received. It is our responsibility to help a mother deal her loss, not hide that loss from her.

Hospitals have the same out-of-sight, out-of-mind policy when it comes to amputated limbs. If a person's limb is amputated at the hospital, doctors and nurses rarely show the limb to the amputee. Of course, we believe that saying good-bye to an amputated limb must be weird, unbelievable, and in bad taste. But one study determined that hospitals can reduce phantom limb pain by 40% by showing the amputated limb to the patient and allowing the patient to say good-bye. Without the chance to say good-bye, the amputee may never come to terms with the fullness of this devastating loss.

Parents and patients who have the chance to say good-bye are better able to process their grief and get on with life. But whenever I suggest that hospitals show amputated limbs to patients and stillborn babies to parents, the staff insist that it would be weird, unbelievable, and in bad taste.

In the case of Sudden Infant Death Syndrome, it is often the mother who gets attention and support while the father is alone with his grief. Friends, doctors, and clergy spend time comforting the mother, but Dad goes right back to work. We imagine he doesn't feel the same flood of emotions the mother feels. We think mothers need more support and care because they have a different, closer bond to their children. That's just not true.

When we deny the bereaved an opportunity to come to terms with their loss, we paint what is often an overwhelming and unrealistic picture for survivors. They never come to know the truth of their loss. Perhaps we do this because we view death and grief as weird, unbelievable, and in bad taste.

The media reinforces this view of death and grief. Recently, a large Midwestern city newspaper ran a picture of a father wailing. The father wasn't just crying, he was wailing; his pain and suffering were obvious. In the background, his home was burning to the ground. The headline read, "Eight Killed in House Fire." Eight of his family members died. This photograph of loss and grief took up half of the front page.

I recall thinking how this photograph was going to upset people in the community. Our society tends to get very upset when grief and mourning are pictured for the world to see. Sure enough, one week later, a letter to the editor appeared in the paper about the photo of the father and his burning house and family.

The reader asked the paper to review its policies concerning good taste in pictorial reporting. She was repulsed by the paper's cheap sensationalism and suggested she would never buy that particular newspaper again. "Your hideous [weird] front page shocker of the grieving father has prompted me to write. Why must you feed people such sickness [unbelievable]? Obviously, your paper lacks imagination and must depend on gory pictures or sickening invasions of privacy to make a buck [in bad taste]."

As you might imagine, a majority of letters from other readers also complained about sensationalism and invasion of privacy.

I've seen plenty of pictures like this, and whenever I do, I must come to grips with my own mortality. I go to my wife and kids, and I give them a hug. Pictures of grief and mourning do something that written words cannot—they force me to live life more fully.

We need to see these pictures, and we need to show the emotions of grieving more openly.

I don't like to see a TV reporter turn the camera on a grieving person, jab a microphone in his or her face, and ask, "Well, how do you feel about this loss?" That's provocation. But no one should be ashamed of displaying grief in public.

People do not like to see pictures of other people grieving. Perhaps they don't want others to know that they, too, are affected by grief. If you view tears as a weakness, you will find photographs like these disconcerting. But pictures show the human side of loss and grief in ways the headlines cannot. They show the reality of grief, whether or not we want to deal with that reality. What if a public display of emotions made some people feel better about displaying grief? Maybe then we could look more closely at our own feelings.

Some people believe that the grieving should be able to select whom they want to share their emotions with. They feel that when the media print stories and pictures representing grief, they are usurping the individuals' right to privacy. Many of us share this opinion, but few ask grieving people how they feel about it. In the case of the man whose family died in the house fire, I followed up.

I called the newspaper that ran the photo and obtained a copy of the story. From the story I got the name of the family and the city where they lived. I obtained the family's phone number from directory assistance and called them.

The man in the picture answered the phone. I told him who I was and what I did for a living, and I asked if he would answer a couple of questions concerning his loss and the subsequent newspaper story and photograph. The man was more than willing.

I asked how he felt about the national coverage his family received in their time of loss and mourning. He answered, "Thank God for that photographer. Because of that photo, in my deepest hour of sorrow, I received over 3,000 responses from people across the United States. I don't know what I would have done without them."

The man went on to say that many people sent his family scripture verses, others sent him books about loss and grief. A nurse from Philadelphia even sent him my business card. He received letters from people who had experienced similar losses in their lives. He got suggestions on what he should and shouldn't do after such a loss. He again told me, "I don't know what I would have done without them."

Grief is a very private emotion, but mourning makes grief public. If this man had not been in mourning, the media wouldn't have taken his picture. Mourning is public; there was no invasion of his privacy.

We all have private thoughts and emotions. But when we make our emotions public, we become responsible for them.

Every time I open my mouth, I become public. This book makes public some of my thoughts and ideas about loss and grief. I need to accept responsibility for my public display, just like everyone else. The man in the picture decided to make his private emotions public. Maybe he knew he would receive comfort. No doubt he needed comforting. When the picture appeared on the front page in papers across the country, it told a lot of other people that they needed to comfort him.

It's a good idea to invade people's privacy once their grief becomes public through mourning. Put your arms around the grieving, and they become more public. Touch them, and they become more public. Ask them about their loss, and they become more public. You aren't invading anyone's privacy, you are allowing someone to be public, to receive the support and comfort they need in order to process their grief.

One of my favorite theories about wailing and moaning is that when we wail and moan, we are trying to get the lost person to come back to us. We are trying to get the one person who can comfort us to hear us. If we cry out loudly enough, maybe what we lost will come back. We learned this in childhood. As a child, if we cried loudly enough, we at least got some comfort.

If you watch people wail and moan at funerals, you will notice that often, all of a sudden, the wailing and moaning stops. It doesn't taper down gradually, it just stops. The next time you see this happen, look to see who just came in through the door.

At one of my lectures, I showed the audience a picture of a man crying in the arms of a priest. Yet it was clear that this man had not been calling out for the priest. I did not know that this same priest was in the audience that day. After my lecture, he came up to me and said, "You know, Dick, you were right. That man cried and cried until his brother's casket came into the room."

Sometimes survivors moan and wail until they see the body of the one they've lost. Seeing the body brings them closure; in effect, it brings the dead person back.

Whenever I hear people complain about the media's portrayal of mourning, I wonder why they don't just turn the page or switch the channel. When someone says, "Last night I watched four hours of that TV special, *Remembering Vietnam*. It was terrible! Just disgusting. There was so much pain. I can't imagine why producers put that garbage on the tube."

We need to see public portrayals of grief and mourning in order to experience the full reality of loss. We need to see it so we can understand how others feel about it. It helps us to cope, to say, "We can survive, because we are not alone in our grief."

A few years ago, when television stations showed the aftermath of the bombing on the marine barracks in Beirut, people in my home state criticized the TV stations. Protesters accused the stations of "infringing on the rights" of family members of soldiers killed in the attack. Some of the stations asked these family members to come into a studio for a town meeting. In an open, live forum, family members talked about their loss and grief. A number of them said they appreciated the news media and the coverage it provided. They were thankful that the reality of their loss was presented and grateful that they had a chance to tell their story to the public. They added that if it hadn't been for the media, they would have been denied the support offered by so many people who would otherwise never have understood their grief.

What is grief counseling all about? Telling the story of a loss. What is a funeral all about? Telling the story of a loss. What was the TV coverage all about?

Media coverage of loss and mourning is like a massive obituary. Sure, there are a few kooks out there who may send letters full of hate or misdirected anger, but most responses from the public are helpful, supportive, and extremely beneficial to the survivors.

We should invade the privacy of grief when we see someone mourning. This can be difficult, because it often means that we will experience some deep, dark, painful feelings ourselves. Grief is highly contagious. If your friend is crying over the loss of her husband, and you go to comfort her, you can feel grief begin to come over you. As you stand close to her, as you open your arms to give her a hug, you catch it completely. When we get upset at the media, it's not because the media is invading the privacy of the survivor, it's because the media is invading *our* privacy. We do not want to get too close to our own feelings of pain and suffering.

You have to admit, it isn't easy to ignore pictures of starving children when they are paraded across the TV screen. My six-year-old son and I were watching a special one night about starving children in Ethiopia. He sat close by me, took my hand, and said, "Daddy, don't make me go there."

When the media invades our privacy as we sit in our living rooms with full stomachs, we often feel motivated to do something, however small. Hopefully, funerals do the same thing. Funeral processions should run right down the main street of town. Invade every onlooker's privacy, and they might just go home, give their kids a hug, and say, "I really love you."

My best friend's wife died of cancer a number of years ago, and I was privileged to be a casket bearer. If you've ever participated in a funeral, you know how funeral directors often separate the casket bearers from their spouses. This funeral was no different. The casket bearers sat at the front of the room, our spouses sat toward the back. On the way to the cemetery, the casket bearers rode in one car, the spouses all went in different cars. At the cemetery, the casket bearers all stood together, the spouses stood separately.

I didn't get any feedback from my wife throughout the funeral. I couldn't check out my feelings or ask about hers. When we rode together to the funeral reception, I finally got to ask her what she thought of the funeral. She said she thought it went really well, except for the way the funeral director closed the casket. She was upset that he didn't pull any curtains; he closed the casket right in front of everybody.

I looked at my wife and said, "Dear, you've had your own curtains in front of your eyes all of your life. They're called 'eyelids.' Why didn't you pull those curtains down?"

She responded, "I don't know. I guess I needed to see what I saw."

When we are confronted with a picture of mourning, whether in the media or in real life, we can look at the floor and examine someone's dirty shoes. We can file our nails, count the squares in the ceiling, or close our eyes and pray. There are countless things we can do, but we watch with wide-open eyes, and then we get upset. We watch because we know we need to see the reality of death, grief, and mourning.

If you are a survivor of a death, you see the casket at the funeral home, and you come to accept part of the fullness of your loss. When you see the casket at the church, and you hear the sermon, you come to terms with more of the loss. As you participate in the burial ceremony at the cemetery and see the casket lowered into the ground, you realize still more emotions associated with your loss. And you may need even more opportunities to work through your emotions. You may have to go back to the grave on an anniversary, on Memorial Day, or on another holiday to search and find the reality of your loss.

Throughout the grieving process, life goes on. Every day you are confronted with life's realities. You have to work through grief, even over the little losses. Think how difficult it would be to face life without the support and strength you gain through each of these small experiences.

In my grief therapy practice, survivors talk about the emotions they experience. Their ability to accept these emotions often depends on whether there was an open or closed casket at the funeral. I think it is essential to have an open casket when-ever physical conditions permit. Some religious groups would take issue with this. To them, viewing the dead body during a funeral is not traditional. However, many of these groups are for-tunate enough to have strong, established rituals—some lasting an entire year—to help survivors work through their grief.

Grief as a Weakness

While grief is often seen as weird, unbelievable, and in bad taste, there is an even more unhealthy view of grief and mourning in society today: grief as a sign of weakness. You've heard people say things like, "And when we told her that her husband died, she just fell apart."

Or, "You know, at the funeral home, she really broke down. And at the cemetery, she just went to pieces."

Or, "I was talking to him about his loss, and he just came unglued."

Falling apart, breaking down, going to pieces, coming unglued—all of these sayings suggest that mourning, the normal expression of grief, is a weakness. My car falls apart, people don't fall apart. Have you ever seen anybody actually fall apart or come unglued? At the funeral home, have you ever heard anybody say, "Excuse me, ma'am, you just dropped your arm"?

Much of my personal experience suggests that the bereaved are afraid that once they start grieving, they will never be able to stop. They fear falling apart, breaking down, going to pieces. Then, even all the King's horses and all the King's men—all the counselors, therapists, nurses, clergy, and doctors—won't be able to put them back together again. Unless you really see someone drop an arm or a leg, never say those words—you will obstruct the healthy process of mourning.

I will never forget watching a man as he learned that his wife had died. As he walked down the hospital corridor, a well-meaning nurse ran to stop him before he entered his wife's room. She told him the sad news, and you could see the grief come over him. It started in his eyes, the wide eyes of disbelief. Then his feet began to fidget. His knees began to shake. I could see his stomach quake and his chest heave. He moved his hand slowly to his eyes. He swallowed hard, his chin started to quiver, and his lips started to strain.

Just then, the well-meaning nurse said, "Go ahead, sir, it's okay to break down." With that, the man dropped his hand, tensed every muscle in his body, and said, "No. No. I'm all right." He remembered the old saying: Get hold of yourself. He got hold of himself because he felt he was going to fall apart, break down, or go to pieces like the nurse suggested. And he wasn't sure anyone would be able to put him back together again.

I don't know if that man ever did cry over the death of his wife. He was stopped from crying in the hall of the hospital, and since then he has probably reminded himself many times that big boys don't cry. He probably learned this childhood lesson too well. Maybe the mourning never came. And when the mourning never comes, that's the beginning of bigger problems that can continue with us for the rest of our lives.

Chapter Four

WORKING THROUGH GRIEF

If you remember one thing from reading this book, I hope it is this: there are no stages in grief. Grief is a process of working to identify what we have lost, the feelings associated with our loss, and who we are now that we've experienced the loss.

Have you ever been invited to go for a ride in a friend's canoe? If you have, chances are you were asked to ride in the front. The person in back steers the canoe, the person in front watches for rocks. The person in back of the canoe controls direction and speed. The person in front just watches the water ahead.

My job as a grief counselor and therapist is to be the person in front, the rider. I am asked to do little more than watch for hazards. Each of us, whenever we are put in a position to offer help and support to a grieving person, is a canoe rider. The grief is not ours. It is the grieving person's canoe. We are only along to watch for the rocks.

If someone who has just been through a divorce says, "I'm going to sell the house tomorrow," that's a rock. If you hear a survivor say, "Gonna take Johnny out of the will. Why, he didn't stay around for more than five days after Dad's funeral," that's a rock, too.

If a recently widowed woman says, "You know, I just met the nicest man in our grief group. I know I've only been widowed for fourteen days and he's only been widowed for thirteen days, but we're thinking about getting married," that's a boulder!

Our job is to be up there at the front of the canoe. The grieving person will steer; we only need to point out the rocks and boulders and waterfalls.

Our partners may want to paddle upstream for a while, and all we can do is remind them which way the current flows. We may be asked to paddle for a bit if they get tired. And when the canoe gets swamped, we won't push it out of the water, we'll pull it to safety. We may be called upon to pull our partners out of the messes they get themselves in as they work through their grief. There ought to be a big sign on grief and mourning: no pushing allowed.

It is dangerous to think of grief as a series of stages. We imagine that we can push survivors through their grief to what we believe is a healthier place, but it will never happen. Grief is a process, as outlined in the illustration on the following page.

The illustration depicts what Dr. William Lamers calls the "Sequential Reactions To Loss." Think of it as a map you can use while you paddle your own canoe of grief or watch for rocks from someone else's canoe. The map will remind you of the many different routes you can take to get from point A to point B.

If you live in New York City, can you get to Jacksonville, Florida, by way of Green Bay, Wisconsin? Yes, you can. Or if you live in San Francisco, can you get to Seattle by way of Mexico City? You bet. There are many different ways to get to the same place. You do not always have to go the shortest route. The shortest route might be boring. Maybe it doesn't offer the best scenery. Maybe you can learn more by taking some detours. Remember, it's your canoe. The route you take as you work through your grief is up to you.

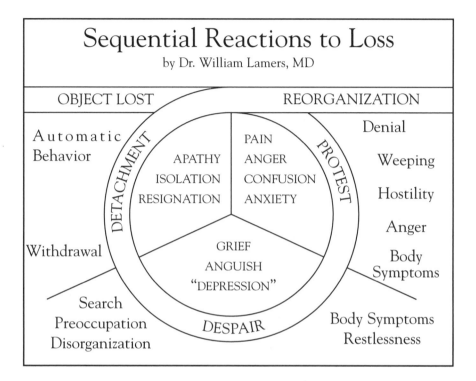

Sequential Reactions to Loss
by Dr. William Lamers, MD

OBJECT LOST · REORGANIZATION

DETACHMENT · PROTEST · DESPAIR

Automatic Behavior · APATHY ISOLATION RESIGNATION · PAIN ANGER CONFUSION ANXIETY · Denial

Weeping

Hostility

Anger

Withdrawal · GRIEF ANGUISH "DEPRESSION" · Body Symptoms

Search Preoccupation Disorganization · Body Symptoms Restlessness

Note that the illustration looks like a road that goes in a circle before it becomes straight. This reminds us that the feelings and behaviors we experience in grief are closely tied. The words inside the circle represent feelings we have as the result of a loss. The words outside the circle are behaviors we exhibit as a result of our feelings. The illustration can help us identify where we are in the grief process—not so we can push ourselves or others through it, but so we can be aware of the rocks that inhibit personal growth.

Protest

Whenever we lose something, whether it's a job, our car keys, or a loved one, our initial reaction will often be to protest the loss.

When a football team loses a down because of an incomplete pass, the team will often protest. Officials in the booth will review the play in instant replay. We do the same thing. Our need to protest a loss is a natural part of the grieving process.

Human beings are pretty lazy creatures. Research suggests that we use only 35% to 40% of our full mental and physical capacity. We protest when confronted with a loss because we know it will take energy to work through our grief. Did you ever hear your parents say, "You spend more energy trying to get out of work than you'd spend if you just did the work?" Well, grief is hard work, and we don't especially want to do it. Loss means change, change means adaptation, adaptation means work, work means expending energy. We don't like to expend energy, so we protest.

Denial is very much a part of protest. But have you ever consider that denial actually signifies acceptance? You cannot deny something without first accepting it. If this confuses you, it's okay, because confusion is the basis of all learning. And since the basis of teaching is clarification, I'll clarify.

Some time ago I hit a dog as I was driving on the highway. I was all alone in the car, and as I pulled off to the side of the road, I said, "Oh no! I couldn't have hit a dog!"

Sounds a lot like denial, doesn't it? "Oh, no! I couldn't have. . . ," but the last words I said gave it away: ". . . hit a dog." I knew what I knew. I didn't say, "Oh, no, I couldn't have hit a giraffe." I knew I had hit a dog. I knew which wheel of my car had hit the dog. And I knew it was very likely the dog was dead. I knew what I knew, but that didn't mean I was ready to accept what I knew.

A few years ago, I had the privilege to counsel an elderly woman named Emma, a patient at a Midwestern medical center. Emma was dying of bone cancer, and she wasn't expected to live much longer than a few months. I saw her every couple of weeks to talk about the feelings she was experiencing as she was dying. She used to say, "Dick, I'm a good die'r, aren't I?"

She was right. I even told her, "Emma, I wish everyone could be as good a 'die'r' as you are."

Emma was in touch with her feelings. She was mentally, physically, and spiritually ready to die, in part because she worked so hard at grieving.

One Saturday morning a nurse from the medical center called me to come talk with Emma. She said, "Dick, you've got to come in and see Emma. I'm afraid she's gone nuts."

"No, not Emma!" was my first response. I knew Emma too well to believe she was going crazy. I went right to the medical center and the nurse met me on Emma's floor.

"I'm glad you got here so quickly," the nurse greeted me. "Get right in to Emma's room and take a look."

I didn't know what to expect. She had been doing so well; at least, that's what I thought. I hesitated briefly, then went to her room.

Here was this dainty, seventy-five-pound woman lying in her big white bed, wearing the biggest sunglasses I had ever seen. She had lost a great deal of weight over the past few months, and the big black sunglasses appeared larger than normal against the white sterile sheets. The first thing I imagined was that Emma must have become extremely sensitive to the light, maybe because of the intensive therapy she had been through. Then I imagined that the stark white room must be one big hazy glare to her. Then I imagined all kinds of things about her that made no sense whatsoever.

I sat down next to Emma and asked how she was doing. She was somewhat surprised that I had dropped in that Saturday morning, but she was glad to see me. We talked for a few minutes. She shared the events of the past few days, and I tried to figure out if she had actually lost touch with reality.

But Emma didn't seem confused. I couldn't imagine what the nurse was talking about. Finally, Emma asked, "Well, how do you like them?"

I said, "What, Emma? How do I like what?"

"My sunglasses, Dick! Didn't you even notice them?"

I told her, yes, I had noticed her sunglasses. I asked if her eyes had been hurting her, with all the bright white in that room. She assured me that her eyes were fine. She had asked the nurse to go to the local drug store to pick up the glasses for her.

"Emma," I asked, "What in the world do you want with sunglasses?"

"Well, Dick," she replied, "I'm going to need them when I go to Hawaii!"

Has there ever been a time in your life when you questioned your abilities? I had thousands of thoughts running through my head. I could not imagine where I had lost this woman. I had believed she was so "together." She knew she was dying. She had worked so hard on her grief. And now, what she said to me sounded like obvious denial. I must have misdiagnosed her somewhere along the line. I could not think how she had slipped by me.

Then Emma asked me about Hawaii. I talked at length about beaches, hot sand, and magnificent sunsets. I talked about luaus, fancy pineapple drinks, and big waves. And all the while I talked, I kept thinking, "Dick, where did you lose this woman?"

Eventually, feeling somewhat frustrated, I excused myself from the room. I desperately needed a break from all the stormy thoughts in my head. As I walked down the hall, I wondered how I could have allowed this to happen. I began questioning my abilities as a counselor, not just with Emma, but with all my clients.

As I gazed out the sixth-floor window over a parking lot full of cars, I wondered if there weren't people down there who would make better counselors than me. I felt a tap on my shoulder and turned to see the nurse who had called me. I'll never forget the biting look in her eyes as she said, "I was just in Emma's room, and I need to tell you, you didn't do her a whole lot of good!"

I was standing there, shaking my head in agreement, ready to apologize for all the years that I had been in this business when the nurse added, "And of all the . . . can you imagine? Why, Emma told me she's just gotten back from Hawaii!"

And then it hit me. A big smile came to my face. You see, while I was thinking about myself, Emma and I were talking about Hawaii. She asked all the questions, I just gave her answers, descriptions, and my own version of what little I knew about Hawaii. And what had looked to me like immense denial on Emma's part was actually great acceptance. Emma knew she was dying. She knew the only way she would ever be able to visit Hawaii was through someone else, someone like me. Imagine Emma accepting that simple fact. She knew how one gets to Hawaii when one is dying. I went straight back into Emma's room and made a date with her for the next evening. When I returned, I brought along a slide projector and all the slides of Hawaii I could find. I brought a boom-box to play Hawaiian music and one of those small, drink umbrellas for Emma's ice water. It was a grand evening—Emma got to visit and enjoy just a little bit of Hawaii.

Three days later, Emma died.

Since that experience, I have been very careful to watch for people's denial, because it is an arrow that points to something they have accepted. And the more obvious the denial, the more profound the acceptance.

When we offer care and support to someone in grief, we need to focus on what has been accepted, forgetting about what is being denied. Denial, in its beginning, is therapeutic. It is only a brief stopover on the rocky road through grief.

Denial is one of the very first behaviors we exhibit to protest a loss. If you were to say that someone significantly close to me just died, my first response would likely be, "No! No! He couldn't have died!" I know that if I looked in your face, I would see that your message was real. Maybe I couldn't handle the reality right then. My next words would probably be, "Tell me you're wrong, you've got to be mistaken!" I would solicit your help in my denial, because I might have trouble accepting the reality of my loss.

We need denial. Denial is a kind of buffer zone, if you will—a place for us to stop so we can take in the reality of the information we know to be true. Denial of a loss isn't all bad; it is our way of preparing ourselves to fully accept our loss and the feelings that come with it.

Some years ago, a woman came to a funeral home where I consulted. I happened to be in the lobby, dressed in a suit and tie. She walked up to me and asked if I was a funeral director. I told her I was (I was a licensed funeral director in Wisconsin). She asked me to come out to her car for a moment. I couldn't imagine what she wanted. As I walked to her car, I looked up and down the street, wondering if maybe I was on *Candid Camera.*

The woman opened the back door of her car, and there lay a beautiful brown and white collie. The woman looked up to me and asked, "Is my dog dead?"

I reached in the car, briefly examined the dog, and told her that as far as I could tell, yes, the dog was dead. I thought perhaps the woman wanted a child's casket or something else she could bury her dog in, but she only said, "Thanks. I just wanted to know if he was really dead." The woman had just come from her veterinarian, who told her that her dog was dead, but that wasn't good enough for her. She said she needed to hear it from someone who specialized in death.

There are levels of denial we can look for as we give care and support to survivors. One is the denial that a loss has taken place. For example, there are survivors who will keep the body of a loved one in their home, telling no one. They will pour lime over the body—a crude sort of mummification process—and lay out the person's clothes every day. They'll cook and do laundry for the person as if he or she were still alive.

Of course, there are subtler ways to deny the loss of a loved one. A survivor might keep the bedroom just the way the deceased liked it, with the same pictures on the wall, the same sheets on the bed, and the same clothes in the closet.

Denial is also evident when one denies or "distances" the full meaning of the loss. For example, a survivor may suggest, "We weren't that close anyway." Or, "Well, I kind of expected this death. It's no big deal."

Some survivors will do away with everything that reminds them of the dead person. They'll take down every picture, and selectively forget significant memories. "Oh, Niagara Falls? I forgot we went there on our honeymoon! Now, how do you suppose I could have forgotten that? Well, I'll be darned."

Some people will deny the irreversibility of death. Such denial may take the form of a spiritual practice or belief: "He's not really dead, he's just in that great workshop in the sky." Denial sometimes involves the occult or séances in an attempt to keep in touch with the dead.

I don't know that there is anything we can do to help the grieving move out of their denial. All we can do is point out the rocks. Whether or not they move their canoe away from a particular rock is their choice.

Another behavior we exhibit in grief is weeping. Weeping can be a beneficial outlet for pain and anger.

Researchers have conducted extensive studies on tears. They have found that the tears we shed from emotional pain are different from the tears we shed from physical pain.

The researchers asked people to sit and watch sad movies, real tearjerkers, like *Brian's Song*. They collected the tears and conducted a chemical analysis. The researchers then exposed these people to eye-irritating chemicals, similar to those found in onions.

When they analyzed those tears, they discovered that the tears contained different hormones.

Anger and hostility are also natural behaviors of people who grieve, and, like weeping and denial, they are manifestations of protest. When something happens that we do not want to accept, we get mad. We blame. When someone dies, we hear, "Damn doctors! If they really knew what they were doing, my mother [or my wife, or my kid] would be alive today!"

Pastor, tell me about your God. I want to know why my loved one is dead. He didn't drink. He didn't smoke. He was a faithful husband. He's dead. And that man down the street does all those terrible things, and he's still alive! Tell me if that's fair. Tell me how God could think that's fair."

"Those damn paramedics. If they'd just been here a few minutes sooner. . . ."

"Damn that funeral director. If he'd never suggested that we view the body, I wouldn't be so sad. He only wanted to make a buck off my grief anyway!"

We even get angry at the dead—really angry, sometimes. But it's not okay to be angry at dead people, so we don't often mention it. Ever hear a widow say she's angry at her dead husband? Widowed people often feel they have been deserted, and that makes them angry. Sometimes that anger is veiled; other times it's more obvious. You might hear a widow say, "When George left me . . . ," as if George had some choice in the matter.

Recently, a widow spoke with me about the death of her husband. I told her that I thought she sounded really angry. "No I'm not angry," she snarled.

I told her it was okay to be angry. It was just a rock I was pointing out, but she couldn't see it. Two sentences later, this woman said, "And do you know how hard it is to get kids to shovel snow? Ninety-five inches of snow this year, and I can't get the kids to shovel the walks! Ninety-five inches of snow and William isn't here to shovel the darned walks!" She was not just a little angry with her husband for dying, she was really angry.

When one of their patients dies, nurses often get angry, too. "Sure, I knew he was dying. But why did he have to die on my shift?" It's the same as saying, "How could he do this to me?"

We feel anger toward ourselves, toward others, toward the dead. But anger doesn't always show itself clearly. Sometimes we kick the dog. Sometimes we quit eating, or we eat foods that are unhealthy for us. We start to have terrible headaches, dizziness, upset stomachs, diarrhea, back pain, neck pain, menstrual problems, forgetfulness, and insomnia. All these are symptoms of anger without an outlet, anger directed at one's self.

Women get a constant message from society that says it's not okay for them to be angry. This is why so many women seek therapy for depression. It's okay for women to be depressed, but not angry. As a result, many women are misdiagnosed and treated for depression.

When I speak in front of a large audience, I like to play a little game of charades. I ask for a volunteer to come to the front of the room, and I whisper a word in her ear that describes an emotion. The volunteer's job is to act out the word to the best of her ability. The audience tries to guess what the emotion is.

The first word I whisper is "anger." The volunteer will make all kinds of angry faces: a tense brow, a frown, clenched teeth. She will angrily fold her arms across her chest and stomp her feet. She will stomp and stomp and stomp until someone in the audience yells, "Anger!"

The second word I whisper is "frustration." The volunteer will make all kinds of sad faces: a furrowed brow, a frown, an open mouth. The volunteer will sadly fold her arms across her chest and step backward: one, two, three steps. No one has fallen off the back of my stage yet; someone will usually yell out, "Frustration!" first.

The third word I whisper is "love." The volunteer will quickly grab me, hug me, and sometimes give me a kiss on the cheek. The audience shouts, "Love!"

Then I whisper a last word in the volunteer's ear. She will stand there with an uncertain look on her face. In all the years I have played this game, not one volunteer has come up with an action to demonstrate this last word. I assure her that she is not alone in her bewilderment, that no one ever gets this word. I thank her, the audience applauds, and I announce that I will try to demonstrate the word myself.

I begin by striking my forehead with my clenched fist. Silence in the audience. I bite my hand. More silence. I kick myself in the rear end, bite my hand, and strike my forehead with my fist, all at the same time (not an easy task, I assure you). Finally, one person in the audience will mumble, "guilt?"

"Guilt!" I seldom ever use that word, but it was the word I was looking for from my audience. Guilt is nothing more than anger directed toward oneself.

We all know about this kind of anger. Whenever we lose something, we tend to get angry at ourselves.

"Dumb me! If only I had taken away his keys, he never would have been driving that car!"

"Dumb me! I should have told him to quit smoking twenty years ago!"

"Dumb me! I could have walked away from that argument, but I had to get right in the thick of it!"

If only.

I should have.

I could have.

And we don't stop with words, do we? We beat ourselves up physically and emotionally to neutralize the pain we feel.

You may not have experienced it firsthand, but you probably know that physical pain neutralizes emotional pain. Physical pain neutralizes physical pain, too. When you wake up in the middle of the night to go to the bathroom, you move quietly, not wanting to wake anyone. You don't turn on the light, you just walk softly next to the bed. Just as you come around the corner of the bed, you drive that little toe of yours right into the edge of the footboard. You've got some serious pain going on in that little piggy, and what do you do? You bite your hand and soundlessly yell, "Arrrggghhh!" Pain neutralizes pain.

Have you ever watched someone take a sliver out of her finger? She will bite her lip, squint her eyes, and gasp to neutralize the expected pain. Have you ever watched a nurse give a patient an injection? He will tense up, bite his lip, and squint as he drives that needle into the patient's arm. Pain neutralizes pain.

When we are in terrible emotional pain, we have a tendency to inflict physical pain on ourselves. When a man loses his job, he might not eat (or he may overeat). When a parent gets upset with her kids, she might get terrible headaches. Many of us get stomach aches and back pains when we experience emotional pain.

Some time ago, a woman came into my office. She had all kinds of physical symptoms—headaches, back pain, tension—all because she was in terrible emotional pain. She was in so much emotional pain that she said to me, "Dick, I'd pay you anything if you could help me get rid of all this emotional pain. I'm just over-whelmed with pain. It's wrecking my relationships, my job, my whole life!" I asked her how much she would be willing to pay me if I could help her get rid of her emotional pain. She said, "Well, I know you can't. But, if you could, I would pay you anything."

"I can help you get rid of your emotional pain," I said. "And I'll guarantee it! Now, how much will you pay me?"

She replied, "Oh, Dick. If you could, I'd pay you whatever amount of money you wanted!"

I asked this woman how much money she had in her check-ing account. She said she had about $2,000 to her name. I told her that for $2,000, I could guarantee that she would leave my office that day with no emotional pain.

With a questioning look, she got out her checkbook and began writing out a check for $2,000. As she began to sign the check, I told her to stop. I told her to tear up the check.

She shook her head with a knowing look on her face, ripping up the check.

"I could help you get rid of all your emotional pain," I explained, "but it would be unethical. All I would need to do is stomp down on your left foot until every bone in that foot was broken. As the paramedics carried you out of my office, I guarantee you would not be feeling any emotional pain!"

The woman glared at me a moment. Then, with wide eyes, she said, "Kitchen cupboard doors!"

Over the past four months, she would periodically open a cupboard door in the kitchen, turn to get something out of the fridge, and when she turned back, whack! She'd bang her head on the door. "You know Dick, those are the moments that I can't recall having any emotional pain!"

People who are grieving tend to be accident prone. They may sprain an ankle, wrench a wrist, cut a finger on a tin can, or slam a hand in a car door. I am always amazed at the number of grieving people who come into my office with bandaged fingers. Each time they return for an appointment, I can almost tell where they are in the grief process by the number of new cuts, bruises, and bandages on their body.

Pain neutralizes pain; it always has and always will. I believe that some people see me, a counselor, as one who inflicts emotional pain. They come into my office with emotional pain, and I challenge them to get in touch with it—a necessary step if one is ever going to work through whatever is causing the pain in the first place.

When the session is over, I open the office door and let my patient go out ahead of me. Many counselors do that. You may think it is because counselors are polite. They may be polite, but they are also watching their backs! Sometimes, when people feel pain, they try to minimize it by directing it at others.

You may have seen people give more money to their church than they could afford after a loved one has died. I know one woman whose three children died in an automobile accident. Afterward, she gave $20,000 to her church. She was frightened that God was sending her a terrible message through the deaths of her children.

In our counseling sessions, we talked about her pain and her reasons for giving so much money to the church. She eventually came to understand that it had nothing to do with some perceived, terrible message from God. If it did, this woman would have had to grieve the loss of her faith as well, because her faith suggested that God would not send such a terrible message. She gave away the money in order to feel great financial pain. This was her way of dealing with the emotional pain. Through counseling, she grew to feel better about herself and her relationship with God. And she began to work through the grief she felt over the loss of her children.

Emotional pain often exhibits itself in physiological symptoms. Research suggests that a high percentage of cases of ulcerative colitis (inflammation of the colon) and osteoarthritis (the degeneration of the cartilage and bone of the joints) appear in individuals who have experienced a recent loss accompanied by unresolved grief.

Recently, psychotherapists have suggested that cancer, too, may be associated with unresolved grief and stress. Therapists interviewed women who had been called back for a second pap smear when the first test proved inconclusive. The women were questioned about any losses they had experienced in the three months to three years prior to the test.

The therapists attempted to predict the results of the women's second pap smear by assessing where these women were in the grieving process. In 77% of the cases, they correctly pre-diagnosed cancer by looking at the women's responses to grief.

Despair

Despair associated with grief is often misdiagnosed as depression. Despair occurs when one loses hope or confidence in a situation. It is a common psychological response to loss.

Depression, on the other hand, is a psychoneurotic or psychotic disorder marked by sadness, inactivity, lack of concentration, difficulty in thinking, a significant increase or decrease in sleep and appetite, feelings of dejection and hopelessness, and sometimes, suicidal tendencies. Whereas depression often requires treatment with psychotherapy or medication, despair does not.

Most of the time, it's fairly easy to tell the difference between despair and depression. Despair (grief) is a kind of emotional see-saw. One minute the bereaved are up, the next minute they are down.

"Oh, I'm so depressed, I can't stand it. But Jim and I are going out tonight, and maybe that will make me feel better. But we're going to that same restaurant where Jack and I used to go, and now, Jack's passed away. But Jim's a nice man, and he has a lot of money. But oh, I feel so down. Maybe things will start looking up someday."

Depression, on the other hand, is a constant down. When people are depressed, little or nothing will get them up. Depressed people will often say things like, "So what? Who cares? Life's just not worth living. I can't sleep, I can't eat. Who could eat at a time like this? Nobody loves me. Guess I'll just go out and. . . ."

When people are bereaved and feeling despair, they appear disorganized. But they are actually organized toward one thing: getting back what they have lost. The jilted lover comments, "I just can't seem to get her out of my mind. Everything I do and everything I see reminds me of her."

The widow may say, "Ah! A paper cup! I remember when Joe drank out of a paper cup just like that one."

A bereaved family member may say, "Look at that light in the ceiling. I can remember when Grandpa had a light in the ceiling just like that one."

Everything reminds survivors of the person they have lost. Many of us have a sense of how they feel, having at some point in our lives lost a boyfriend or girlfriend.

I will never forget the first time I was "dumped." I became very disorganized. My school work suffered. I started seeing less of my friends. I began to come home late, past my curfew, because I had to drive by her house thirty or forty times every night. Each song I heard on the radio happened to be "our song." All of my energy was focused on one thing—getting back what I had lost.

When survivors say, "I just can't seem to get him out of my mind," it is because they don't want to. If you have ever experienced a significant loss in your life, such as the death of a loved one, you have probably dreaded having to grieve over all the little things that remind you of your loss.

No one wants to experience more grief than necessary. When we lose someone physically, we do not want to lose that person emotionally, too. Working through grief is not fun. Everything reminds us of what we have lost, and we hope we will never have to let go and get busy with the work of grieving.

When we can't get someone out of our mind, people tell us to "just keep busy." But keeping busy doesn't help, does it? In fact, it can do more harm than good.

Let me give you an example. I want you to keep reading for a while; do not put this book down, even though someone has just run into your car.

I know you didn't hear the crash, because you were so engrossed in this book. Just keep busy reading, even though the driver totaled your car. And he's speeding away! Can you believe that?

Don't look now, but the driver has stopped at the end of the street to check out the damage to his own car. You could probably run out and get his license plate number, but don't—just keep concentrating on what you are reading. Your car has been totaled by a hit-and-run driver who is parked just down the street, but you should just keep busy reading.

"Don't look now" is the oldest hypnotic trick in the business. What happens when someone tells you something like, "Don't think about the position of your left foot. Don't notice that your left shoe is feeling tighter and tighter?"

When we are faced with the death of a loved one, and someone tells us, "Don't think about Bill (or Sue, or Aunt Mary, or Grandpa), just keep busy," what are we likely to do? The only words we remember are *think about Bill*. This is what hypnosis is all about. We do this to each other every day. We scream at our kids, "Don't run into the street!" And where is the first place they run to?

"Don't be late!"

"Don't do drugs!"

"Don't have sex!"

To see how well this strategy works, just look at the kids in our world today. It would be better to be honest:

"You can have sex, but let me tell you how I feel about it. Let me try to help you understand the truth and consequences of sex."

"You want to do drugs? If you want to, I cannot stop you. But I can tell you what I know about drugs."

"When you come home late, I worry about your safety and I can't get to sleep when I go to bed. If I don't sleep because I'm worried about you, I suffer. I don't like to suffer, so please don't come home late."

"You can't get your mind off Bill? I know, it's tough to accept the fact that Bill is dead. It hurts. I love you, and I don't want you to feel pain, but you do. All I know is, I miss Bill, too. And I need a hug."

If we appear disorganized in our grief, it is because we are organized toward one thing. We do not want to make big decisions. In our grief, life overwhelms us. That is why, when someone close to us is grieving a major loss, it is important that we help wherever we can by pointing out the rocks. This often means we must help the grieving make important decisions in their lives. The grieving may call upon us to help them organize their thoughts as they move closer to accepting the truth of their loss.

When people are bereaved, they also appear restless. We see the restlessness, agitation, and chaos, and maybe this is why our advice is, "Just keep busy." We all do some of our best work when we are restlessly busy doing other things, don't we?

When we drive a car, we don't think, "Uh-oh, a corner coming. Better push the brake pedal two-and-a-half inches. The vehicle is now slowing. . . . Brake another half inch. Now turn the wheel a bit to the left. Lift the brake half an inch."

No one drives like that. Instead, we do some of our best and safest driving when we are not thinking about every move we make. We leave our conscious mind open so we can react to situations on the road as they present themselves.

In the meantime, our minds are busy doing other things. But when our minds are too busy, we sometimes do strange things. Have you ever run a red light without realizing it? If you have, you were thinking of something entirely unrelated to driving, and that took up your concentration.

When people have thinking to do, they sometimes clean. I have seen people clean everything in the house and then start on the garage. By getting busy, they are able to do some of their best thinking.

When someone we care about is grieving a major loss, it is important to tell him or her to "get busy." *Keeping* busy will accomplish nothing. *Getting* busy—getting to work on grieving—will help the survivor accomplish a lot. "I know, it hurts! It's hard for you to concentrate on anything else. But if you get busy, you can start to work through your grief." Getting busy on your grief, recognizing what you have lost and how you feel about it, is a necessary task.

When an employee experiences the death of an immediate family member, most businesses will give that employee some days off, with or without pay. Although it's a wonderful gesture on the employer's part, the fact is, employers know that bereaved employees aren't worth a damn on the job. They are often emotionally or physically unable to do their work. They are also more prone to injury. Bereaved employees will not be thinking clearly, and they could be a source of accidents.

Have you ever noticed how people have a tendency to pace in their grief? Pacing serves an important purpose. It is a way for the bereaved to act out the searching that often follows a loss.

Restlessness is a part of searching. Whenever we lose something, we attempt to recover it. Think about the search that goes on when you lose something as simple as your car keys. It's a ritualistic search. First, you pat all of your pockets: front pants pockets, back pants pockets, jacket pockets, shirt pockets. You look at your empty, outstretched hands with bewilderment.

Next, you reach in and explore the trinkets in each of those pockets: front pants pockets, back pants pockets, jacket pockets, shirt pockets. Again, you look at your empty, outstretched hands with bewilderment. Then you start patting down your pockets all over again, then searching through your pockets, and so on. This ritual can go on for ten minutes.

Let's say you lose a pair of scissors. Yours eyes dart across the countertop as you move to one end of the counter. You open the first drawer. No scissors. You move on to the second drawer. Still no scissors. On to the third drawer, then the fourth, and on and on to the last drawer.

If you do not happen to find the scissors, what do you do? Your eyes dart across the countertop as you step back to the end of the counter. You proceed to search through every drawer again in the same ritualistic order as before.

Whenever we lose something, we launch a formal or ceremonial process to find it. A man who has lost his wife due to death might, in the middle of the night, go for a drive. He will hop in the car, back out of the driveway, and go. Afterwards, if you ask him where he went, he will answer, "Oh, I don't know. I just drove." Take out a city map and ask him to show you where he drove. Chances are he drove by the restaurant he and his wife used to go to every Wednesday night. Or he just happened to drive by the church they both went to worship every week. And chances are good that his drive took him by the cemetery where his wife is now buried.

When a survivor searches for the person he or she has lost, chances are that the search will eventually take him or her to the cemetery. The survivor might take the long way, but he or she will end up there eventually. The sad thing is, most of our cemeteries are locked at night.

We are told that cemeteries are locked to keep kids from vandalizing them. I think there is a reason that kids want to go to the cemetery at night. There they can get close to death. They can sit on the graves, drink beer, turn over stones, and emerge unscathed. "Ha ha! See what I did? And Death didn't get me!" This can be educational. Kids need to learn that death is not lurking around the corner, waiting to get them. Instead of waiting for kids to break into a locked cemetery, why don't we take them there on a school field trip? It would help them learn about the reality of death. Why not? Because that would be weird, unbelievable, and in bad taste.

We all search for the meaning of death. We search for ways to overcome death. We search in an attempt to regain what we have lost. But in our futile investigations, we miss a more important search: the search for life, for what it means to be alive, for ways to live before we die.

When we search for the loved ones we have lost, we aren't exactly sure where our search will take us. All we know is that we *must* search in order to work through our grief. *How* we search is not as important as the result of the search.

People often ask if I think it is healthy for survivors to view the body of the dead. I have always answered that it's not only healthy, it's imperative. "But Dick," someone will ask, "it was suicide. One shotgun blast to the head, you know. How can you expect the survivors to view the body?"

I respond, "What part of the body can the survivors view? Can the head be covered while the dressed torso is left uncovered?"

"Well, we'll just put up a picture of the recently departed. That will be so much easier."

Easier for whom? The funeral director? Or the family member who does not want to accept the loss? Or the relative who doesn't want everyone to know the real nature of the death? Who are we trying to fool? Who are we hurting when we deny the full reality of a suicide? The answers become all too clear when, three months after the funeral, one of the family is found searching a dark cemetery after driving around town all night.

If I happen to die in a car accident, and the funeral director cannot show my face because of the nature of my fatal injuries, I would hope—for my grieving wife's sake—that he or she would wrap my face in gauze and display the rest of my body. I am confident that my wife would recognize my hands, my jewelry, my clothes.

When survivors see the hands, the watch, the ring, familiar clothing, scars, tattoos—anything to identify their loved one—they begin to come to terms with their loss. Part of the search is over. The reality of the loss begins to set in, and the remaining work of grief commences.

A few years ago, I came to know a family who had lost their father to drowning. The funeral director in charge of the arrangements made a somewhat frantic call to me. He said the family wanted to view the body and there was nothing that could be done to make the deteriorated body presentable. I suggested that he do whatever he could and then let the family view the body. He agreed, on the condition that I be there when family members arrived.

As the family got out of their cars in front of the funeral home, I could tell that some of them had been drinking heavily. In fact, an older man, the man's brother, was quite drunk. The family entered the funeral home and gathered at the back of the viewing room. The drunken man stumbled toward the open casket, calling his brother's name over and over. He began to yell and curse. He cursed his brother, the police, the medics, and himself. Finally, he leaned over the open casket and touched his brother's body. He stopped crying and cursing. Turning toward me, he said, "Boy, my brother really looks dead, doesn't he?"

Even in a state of drunkenness, this man used all his senses to come to terms with what he knew. He saw. He touched. He smelled. Now he knew his brother was dead. Even though he was drunk, this man no longer had lingering questions about his brother being dead.

About twenty years ago, I received another call from a director. He said that a mother had come to him and desperately wanted to see her son's body. The problem was, her son had been dead for twenty-eight years, and never buried. Apparently, he had been shot down over a jungle in China in 1945, and the airplane and body had only recently been discovered.

I said that I didn't understand what the problem was. The funeral director responded, "Dick, that woman doesn't want to see the body. I know she doesn't."

He had portions of the body—a skull, arm bone, and a few other small bones—and the man's dog tags. "She tells me she needs to see the body. But Dick, she doesn't want to see this body." I reminded him that he already told me that, but the fact was, the woman needed what she said she needed.

The funeral director believed that he knew what the woman wanted, but he obviously didn't hear her say what she needed. In some cases, survivors may not want to view a dead body, although it might be something they desperately need to do. This woman said she needed to see her son's body. Who are we to say any different?

The funeral director agreed to show this woman the remains of her son, and we laid out the remains before she arrived. I put the skull on the pillow inside the casket, the miscellaneous bones in their respective places, and the dog tags right up front. When the woman got to the funeral home, she proceeded directly to the casket. She touched the skull, carefully moved her hand across one of the bones, and picked up the dog tags. She looked up to me and said, "Thank God, it's over. After twenty-eight years, it's finally over!"

For twenty-eight years, every time the doorbell rang, every time the phone rang, every time the mail carrier stopped by her mailbox—every day, for twenty-eight years, she thought she would hear from her son. Now the waiting was over.

We see how important it is for families to have the remains of their loved ones returned from Vietnam to the United States. Families will grieve beside caskets containing the remains of their brother, father, or son who has been missing in action for twenty-two years. After all these years, the survivors are still working through their grief.

Survivors of death will search until they come to understand their loss. Searching is to be expected; it is part of working through grief. But our society tends to treat searching the same way we treat death—as weird, unbelievable, and in bad taste.

In the suburb of a large Midwestern community, a woman was arrested for trespassing in a cemetery. She climbed over the fence at 2 A.M. Police found her crying over the grave of her husband. I just happened to be at the courthouse when the case was called, and I had an opportunity to speak with the judge. I explained why this woman was in the cemetery at night. I told him that we should unlock cemetery gates and provide security for survivors who have the need to search as they work through their grief. The judge spoke with the woman and dismissed the case.

It is not just family members who may need to search. Nurses sometimes need to search, too. If a nurse comes into work at 2 A.M. and hears, "Mr. Evans died last night," the response is often, "No! Mr. Evans? Are you sure?" (Denial.) "But he was doing so well. You're mistaken, aren't you?" (It must be a mistake.) Eventually, "Mr. Evans really died, huh? I told that dumb doctor to change his meds. If only he'd listened to me." (Blame and anger.) Then, "Wasn't anybody watching him? If only I'd been here, this never would have happened." (Anger directed at self—what society calls "guilt.")

Then the nurse gets a queasy stomach, the I've-got-to-sit-down-a-minute blues. He or she becomes disorganized: "Er, do I start in on my shift? Should I start with meds, or give baths? . . ." Eventually the nurse meanders by the dead patient's room and glances in. Maybe he or she stops, pushes the door open a bit, and cautiously walks into the room. Nine times out of ten, the bed is empty. The dead body has already been moved down to the morgue. Or worse, another patient is already lying in the bed.

I don't envy the new patient. If the nurse had any kind of relationship with the one who died, he or she will feel some anger. The anger might be directed toward the man or woman now lying in that bed. I have suggested that hospitals try to keep a bed empty for at least twenty-four hours after a patient has died. This would give the staff—who, by the nature of their work, have made tremendous investments in the lives of their patients—time to come to terms with the reality of the loss. Most hospitals tell me they just can't do that. It is not economically prudent.

Then I suggest that hospitals offer their staff classes on loss and grief. I am told that nurses get plenty of instruction on death and dying in college; there's no need to talk about loss and grief. That would be weird, unbelievable, and in bad taste.

So nurses search. Doctors search. Volunteers search. These survivors may not know they do it or why they do it, but they search, and they ask, "Why?"

"Why"—a small word with great significance. Members of the clergy hear that word a lot. "I just want to know, Pastor. Why? Why my child? Why my loved one? Why me? What did I ever do to deserve this?" Survivors often look to themselves for the answers. Many people believe that if they are good, then good things will happen to them. The death of a loved one must mean they are bad.

In his book *When Bad Things Happen to Good People*, Rabbi Harold S. Kushner points out that people who feel they are being punished for their past deeds are usually religious. They search through their past with a religious microscope to discover some sin that will explain why this bad thing happened to them. Of course, everyone will die at some point, and our misdeeds or sins are not the cause of death. It may help survivors to remember that both good and bad things happen to all people.

I love to see pictures of people searching near the Vietnam Memorial in Washington, D.C.—America's own Wailing Wall. There are 58,022 names engraved in 275 stone blocks. Soon there will be a monument to include those who are missing in action. Why? Because we want to help survivors in their search for the people they have lost.

You may have noticed that the Vietnam Memorial was designed to stand apart from the walkway in front of the monument. There used to be a small strip of grass between the stone monument and the walkway. Park staff say that the little strip of grass was probably the most frequently replaced grass in America. The grass has since been replaced by stone. When someone searches the wall for a friend or loved one, no strip of grass—or barrier of any kind, for that matter—will keep them from getting as close as they can to finding what they have lost.

Many veterans search the memorial in their camouflage uniform, the kind of clothes they wore during the war. They know that when you are searching for a buddy, you should at least wear the kind of clothes your buddy would recognize.

After they find the name they are looking for, most searchers get a piece of paper, place it across the inscription, and create a pencil rub of the name inscribed in the black stone.

We seem to need stones when there has been a death. If there are huge deaths, there are huge stones. If there are many deaths, there are many stones. We go to these stones to search. We mourn at these stones. Searching happens even more often when the bodies have never been viewed, like the bodies of many soldiers who died in Vietnam.

We erect stones in order to search. We take rubbings of the inscriptions and we bring those rubbings home. Some people frame their rubbings and hang them in their homes so they will know that their loved ones have died. This is why we make cemetery stones out of marble and granite. The stones will be around forever, long after the memories of our loved ones are gone.

When survivors need to search, they need to know where to go. This is very important. Attending the burial at the cemetery often serves as the survivor's final search; it is a necessary part of working through grief. In some northern communities, however, the ground is frozen for months at a time. Burials frequently have to wait until the spring. By then, only a few close family members are present, if even that. Many of the survivors never experience the valuable lessons learned in the search that takes them to that final destination.

In some places, bad weather is enough to deny survivors the experience. "Oh, it's raining. Let's just conclude here at the church (or funeral home). No need to go on to the cemetery." I hope funeral directors, clergy, and family understand that, for some, the search will not end there.

Detachment

Detachment is another place we visit as we travel the road of grief. It is an exhausting place. Detachment is where we finally say, "I've had enough of this pain."

It is the point in our grief work where we decide, "I've gone through so much of this 'processing' stuff . . . I'm sick and tired of being sick and tired. I quit!"

Detachment works a lot like a taffy machine. The machine stretches the candy, pulling until you think it's about to break, then it wraps it up again. Stretch, pull, fold, stretch, pull, fold.

The widower says, "I'm tired of this pain. I quit." Then he hears that song again on the radio and is reminded of his wife.

"I've dealt with Dad's death, and I feel much better, thank you." But when the daughter drives by Dad's favorite restaurant, all the feelings come welling back up inside.

Just when you think you're all done with your divorce, he comes by to pick up the kids. And he looks good.

There may come a time when we say to ourselves, "I'm sick of this," and so we withdraw.

Withdrawing means backing away from other people—into our home, into the TV, into the bedroom with the TV, into a bottle of booze. When we detach, we sometimes withdraw from churches, clubs, jobs, and all social activity. We back into ourselves.

Health care professionals know about withdrawing. If a patient is going through painful treatment, it isn't a good idea to let that patient close his or her eyes during the procedure, because the pain will be internalized.

When we feel pain, we tend to pull inside, close our eyes, and wrap ourselves up in a tight little ball. We think this means security, but we should actually do just the opposite. We need to open up when we feel pain; otherwise there will be no place for the pain to go but inside. Opening up allows us to get the pain out.

Men, in particular, tend to withdraw. We withdraw into our work. We work like crazy when we feel pain. It doesn't matter if we are physicians from Sheboygan, janitors from Jacksonville, or preachers from Los Angeles, we will work like madmen all day long, have a couple of stiff drinks at night to help us sleep, and wake up the next day to do the same thing all over again. We think that if we work hard enough, in six or eight months we'll be over our grief. Plus, we'll get rewarded for all our hard work. We will make more money and maybe even earn a promotion, as well as the praise of all our friends.

"Hey, isn't old Dick handling the death of his wife quite well? I mean, look at him. Only two weeks, and he's right back in the old saddle! Attaboy, Dick!"

And if that doesn't work, we'll just increase the dose of work or alcohol.

When confronting major losses in our lives, some detachment can be quite healthy. The trouble comes when we detach *too* much. Working a little harder may be healthy (remember, get busy), but working too much harder will create additional problems. Having a drink to help us sleep at night may be healthy, but drinking too much will create additional problems. We can end up completely absorbed in ourselves, withdrawing to the point of no return. And all the while we are putting off the work we need to do to process our grief.

When we see people withdraw into their work, hobbies, drinking, or any other behavior, the most we can do is tell them about the rocks we see. We can ask ourselves if their behavior is typical for them, given their circumstances, and whether it helps or hinders them as they try to get in touch with reality.

One thing I find terribly hard to do as a counselor is work with drunken little old ladies. I see more drunken little old ladies than you can imagine. And each one of them is someone's grandma. It never gets any easier to talk to them or their families about their behavior. More and more widows are withdrawing into alcohol.

Family members tell me, "Dick, you're a nice man. And we certainly trust you. Everything you've said to us has been right on target. But Dick, you're wrong on this one. Grandma can't be a drunk!" Nevertheless, I have to point out the rock.

In the Upper Midwest, people have a marvelous way of helping survivors deal with withdrawing. I call it the Jell-O Brigade.

When a loved one dies, the Jell-O Brigade get out their very best dishes—no cracks, chips, or dents—whip up their best salads, pies, cakes, cookies, and casseroles, and take them to the bereaved. It's ingenious.

The Jell-O Brigade does two things. First, it force-feeds the survivors. These cooks don't prepare just one helping of goulash or two small pieces of cake, they make several meals. The survivors' counters are so full of pies, cakes, and cookies, their refrigerators are so full of casseroles, desserts, and home-baked breads, there is hardly room to store the leftovers.

Survivors frequently say they don't need all that food. They aren't hungry, that don't have time to eat, people shouldn't have gone through all that work—but they will eat what you bring them. Basic Midwestern values tell them they just can't let all that food go to waste while kids are starving in Ethiopia. And this ritual gives the soldiers of the Jell-O Brigade the opportunity to extend their condolences along with some compassionate, helping hands.

But the Jell-O Brigade accomplishes something even more important. Four days after the funeral, the widow sits at home, sipping coffee at the kitchen table, praying to her God that she will die. "This is hell, Lord. I don't know how I'll live without him. Just let me die, too."

But when she's done praying, she looks up from her steaming coffee, wipes the tears from her eyes, and sees all those dishes—her friends' best silver trays, favorite casserole dishes, and precious crystal cake platters. It's like a bolt of lightning. She pleads, "Wait, Lord. Hold on just a minute. I can't die yet!"

The widow has to return the dishes. She has already washed them, although she can't recall when or how. But that doesn't matter. What matters is the widow will load her friends' dishes into her car and personally return them, one at a time.

And at every house, she begins, "Oh, I don't know how to thank you. I just didn't have the energy to cook, and you were so thoughtful!"

"No problem. It's the least I could do. Can you come in for a cup of coffee?"

"Well, I have so much to do . . . I don't know. . . . Well, I guess so, just for a minute."

The first thing the friend asks is, "How are you doing?"

Up until now, the widow has felt alone in her grief. True, her friends visited. Her priest, minister, or rabbi stopped by every day. The kids came home; she was surrounded by relatives. She never seemed to have a moment alone. It would have been difficult for anyone to have a private conversation with her over the past few days. But now she can talk.

She talks about her grief, her pain, her loneliness. "It's been hell. You just don't know, it's pure hell. Nobody else seems to understand. All of my friends still have their spouses. No one seems able to relate to me. Other widows are so much older, and I just can't relate to them. It's so empty around the house. I can't sleep in that bed; I go to sleep in the recliner every night. There are sounds in the house that drive me nuts; every time I hear them I think that it's him. And there are certain smells that remind me of him, too, and I turn around, but he's not there. He's gone, isn't he?"

She cries, and the two friends hug each other as their coffee gets cold. After an hour or two, the widow leaves to return the rest of the dishes. And at every friend's house she stops for coffee. And with every friend she talks, cries, and hugs. The friends listen, offering soft shoulders and more hugs. This is the best thing that could happen for the grieving widow, or for anyone bereaved.

In big cities today, it seems that people just don't have time for the Jell-O Brigade. Instead, the bereaved go to therapists. Hopefully, these therapist are able to help the bereaved talk so they can hear themselves redefine who they are now, after their loss.

Communities that still have the Jell-O Brigade are on the verge of muddling it up, because friends are beginning to deliver food on disposable pie tins and paper plates. Please don't do this. When you take food to survivors, use your best china, your best silver, your most precious dishes, even family heirlooms. Don't worry—the bereaved will know how precious these dishes are to you. They will return them, personally.

And the bereaved will probably take the time to have a cup of coffee, if you invite them in. They will tell the story of their grief over and over again, as long as they have dishes to return. They will begin to come to terms with the full reality of their loss. Each time survivors tell their story they will cry, and they will receive comfort. And each time, the loss will become easier and easier for them to accept.

Never offer to return dishes for survivors. Let them do it on their own. Important healing will happen; it will help end their desire to withdraw. It will accomplish, in a reasonable period of time, what would otherwise take months at a counselor's office.

Reorganization

As I've suggested, grief is the process of identifying:

- the full reality of a loss we've incurred
- the feelings that result from that loss
- who we are after the loss

Once the bereaved have worked through these issues, they will begin to exhibit signs of reorganization of self.

The first sign of reorganization is when the bereaved are able to talk out loud about their loss.

"I got divorced."

"I lost a leg."

"My spouse died."

"My child died."

The bereaved begin to verbalize the truthfulness of the loss. They use the words "I" and "me" more frequently. They say "divorced" instead of "separated," "died" instead of "passed away."

Sometimes the words come quickly after a loss, sometimes it takes awhile. When they start to come, it's a sign that the grieving have begun to reorganize their lives, to identify who they are now, after their loss.

Another sign of reorganization is when the bereaved can talk about the fullness of their loss, and not become emotionally overwhelmed. Their lives are different now, but life does go on.

"My wife died. She had an illness, a terrible illness. I remember the day she died. I took her to the hospital, and. . . ." You might see tears in the eyes or a lump in the throat, but the survivor continues talking about the loss. It might be six years later or sixty, but the bereaved is no longer overwhelmed by his or her emotions.

Another sign is when the bereaved can talk realistically about the loss or the person who died. Saints tend to be born immediately after a death. "Oh, he was a perfect husband, a great man. I'm telling you, there was no one kinder, gentler, . . ."

A little while into the grieving process, you might hear, "Yes, he was a wonderful man." The description goes from "perfect" to "wonderful." After a little more time (and hard work), it becomes, "He was a fine man." Then, "He was a good man, but I'll never forget the time he. . . ." As the bereaved moves through her grief, you learn that she was married to a full human being, and the marriage was somewhat less than perfect.

After a divorce, the process is reversed. First it's, "Yeah, well I hope the sucker gets hit by a truck! I've always hated his guts, that no-good scum!" After a while, "Oh, we had a rotten marriage, all right. Things weren't that good. But I'll tell you, he was good with the kids." But when reorganization begins, all of a sudden it's, "You know, compared to some of the doorknobs I'm running into at those single meetings, he wasn't all that bad!" You hear the bad, the good, and the in-between.

Another sign of reorganization is when the bereaved begin to feel good about feeling good.

About three months after my father died, I asked my mother how she was doing. Her eyebrows tensed up, her lips drew tighter, and she said, "I think I'm doing much better, now."

"Mom, why do you say that?"

"Well, it's like the other night. I was watching the Carol Burnett Show and that crazy Tim Conway did his old-man shuffle. I was sitting there, watching, and I started to laugh. Then I thought, 'Oh my God, it's only been three months.' " My mother was coming to terms with the fullness of her loss, and she was beginning to feel better. But it still wasn't okay to be feeling too good. It wasn't okay to laugh just yet.

Nine months later, I again asked my mother how she was doing. She raised her eyebrows, smiled, and said, "Oh, I'm doing much better now. You know, just the other night, the gals and I went out for dinner. We played some bingo, drank a little wine, told a few stories, and I got the giggles. I didn't get home until about eleven o'clock. As I was getting undressed for bed, I realized that my sides hurt from laughing so hard. I sat there and said to myself, 'Boy, that sure feels good!' "

There was a little tear in her eye when she said, "that sure feels good." There was some sadness in her voice, too. But she felt good about feeling good.

When the bereaved can eat and taste and enjoy their food, it is a sign they are feeling good about feeling good. When they hear a song that reminds them of the person they have lost, tears might come to their eyes, but they still enjoy the song. When they walk in the park and hear a familiar bird call and are reminded of the past, a smile comes to their face because they remember good feelings they shared with their loved one. The bereaved begin to feel good about feeling good.

You begin to see the return of sexual behaviors, when the bereaved can feel good about feeling good sexually. Widows in particular do not like to talk about these feelings. In counseling, when I ask a widow how she is doing, she might say, "Oh, I'm getting some of those same feelings back again."

"What feelings?"

"Oh, Dick, you know."

"No, I don't know. What feelings are you talking about."

She'll smile, bow her head, and say, "Those feelings." It's a beginning, a sign that it is okay to feel good about feeling good.

Sexuality creates all sorts of problems for couples when their child has died. The two bereaved people will never be at the same place in their grieving. Both had a different kind of investment in the child they lost. Both have different ways and times of working through their grief. It is almost as if they orbit each other; when one is down, the other is up.

One day, Dad is down in Sewer City with his grief, and Mom doesn't want to go down there because she knows how painful it is. So Mom stays away from Dad. The next day, Dad's up, feeling good about feeling good, and Mom is in the dumps. Dad signals that he is ready for some affection, and Mom says, "Are you crazy? Don't you know I'm hurting? How can you think about sex at a time like this?"

Mom and Dad are both bereaved, but they are working through their grief individually, and they are never in the same place at the same time. How often are a couple in the same place emotionally, even when they're not grieving? Have you and your partner ever had your eyes meet, your hands touch, and just known it was time, so you made mad, passionate love in the dining room at the Howard Johnson's? No, it doesn't work that way. Two people are seldom in the same emotional place at the same time.

Couples experiencing pain and grief are often worlds apart. Mom and Dad distance each other in grief because they are not the same people they were before their loss. Mom and Dad are different now; they have changed. Both are redefining who they are now, after their loss.

Research shows that nearly 80% of all couples whose children die of leukemia will divorce or come close to divorcing, within one year of their child's death. This happens, in part, because of unresolved grief. Mom and Dad will need to confront themselves, as they are now, both individually and within their relationship. They will need to talk about the changes that have occurred in their relationship, and their friends will have to be there for them.

As the friends of a grieving couple, we can point out some of the rocks in their way. We cannot take away the pain. We cannot bring back what is lost. But we can assure the grieving couple that they can work through their grief, if they redefine themselves, individually and as a couple, after a major loss. We can encourage couples to talk about all aspects of their relationship, and maybe see a counselor to help them sort things out.

Another sign of reorganization is when the bereaved begin to interact with new people, joining new clubs, new groups, and new organizations. Clergy sometimes get upset if a bereaved individual moves to another place of worship. They feel that he or she is leaving them personally. But what the bereaved is often saying is, "This old church won't let me be Sally Smith. It wants me to stay Mrs. John Smith, but that's not who I am anymore."

We must take care to distinguish between actions that indicate anger or withdrawal and actions that signify real growth. When survivors of a recent death say they are leaving their church or synagogue, ask them why. Are they leaving because other members won't let them be the person they are now, or is it something else entirely? Are they angry at God, or maybe their rabbi, pastor, or priest?

Recently, a woman I counseled said she was leaving her church. When I asked why, she said that for seven Sundays since her husband died, she went to the same early-morning service, sat in the same pew that she and her husband had always sat in, and put the same amount of money in the collection box. But not once had the pastor approached, called, or visited her to talk about the death of her husband. I suggested that she talk to her pastor before she left the church. Perhaps her pastor did not know she needed his support.

A couple of weeks later, she spoke with the pastor. "But I probably could have done it in a better way," she said. "Last week, after the service, I went up to shake the pastor's hand, and said, 'Nice sermon, pastor. By the way, did you notice Henry wasn't with me?' "

The pastor thought she was going crazy, so he called her up the next Tuesday to talk about her loss. He also spoke of the loss that he felt. The pastor was grieving, too. He was in a process of reidentifying who he was now that Henry was dead. He had invested love, affection, kindness, and caring into his relationship with the woman's dying husband, and he did not want to be reminded of the loss. The widow and her pastor have a closer relationship now, because they were able to share their individual losses.

Sometimes I think the clergy should be sitting in the front row at the funeral with the family instead of standing behind the podium delivering the sermon. Too often, clergy members have personal relationships with the dead, and they have to work through their grief just like the rest of us.

Dating or remarrying can also be signs of reorganization. I advise survivors not to remarry for at least a year. Reidentification takes hard work, and hard work takes time. Many events—birthdays, anniversaries, holidays—will take place during that year for the first time without the loved one. Each event will bring the bereaved new realizations of loss, new feelings that result from this loss, and questions about who they are now.

Many widowed or divorced people will redecorate their home right after a loss. This, too, can be a sign of reidentification. Divorced individuals often get rid of the bedroom set, which is not always a bad idea. But burning the bed? Now there's a rock.

Sometimes the recently divorced will change the curtains, furniture, or kitchen cabinets. Sometimes they will sell their house. I advise people to use caution when making major changes soon after a divorce, but they must make their own decisions. The number of healthy changes that can happen often depends on the seriousness of the loss.

Tasks of Mourning

According to J. William Worden, there are four major tasks of mourning that must be accomplished by the bereaved. The first is to accept the reality of our loss. Society may want us to believe that our loved one has expired, passed on, or bought the farm, but the truth is that he or she has died. We will need to accept the natural law that says he or she is gone and will never return; there will be no reunion in this life.

The state tells us that when a marriage is dissolved, we are married no longer. We are not separated, apart, or having disagreements; we are divorced. We cannot expect to receive a tax deduction, help around the yard, help with the dishes, or sexual gratification from our spouse. We are no longer married. The sooner we come to terms with our loss, the sooner we begin to redefine ourselves.

No matter what the loss, anything that you and I can do to assist the bereaved in accepting this loss will help them in their recovery from grief. Talking about death, comforting the survivors, encouraging a truthful view of death, and remembering the death for weeks, months, even years from now will help the bereaved address the reality of their loss.

The second task of mourning is to experience the pain of our grief. Collin Murray Parkes stated, "Anything that continually allows a person to avoid or suppress the pain of a loss can be expected to prolong the course of mourning."

When we are grieving, we will try anything to avoid pain. One of my clients masturbated every time his pain became too evident, and that was twenty to thirty times every day. Some people get into bizarre sexual relationships because they are trying to avoid feeling the full pain of their loss. It has less to do with sex than with trying to stop the thoughts that bring about their pain.

We try to avoid pain by idealizing the dead. It takes tremendous work to portray our dead loved one as a perfect saint, and in that hard work we can avoid the pain. We can also work hard to make a devil out of the dead. "No big deal. He was a real jerk, anyway. Doesn't bother me a bit that my friend died."

We might move to a different city to avoid the pain, but it doesn't work for long. We know this, but we move anyway. By moving, we hope there will be fewer things to remind us of our loss and cause us pain. The problem is, the pain of working through our grief follows us.

If we are ever to work through our grief, it is imperative that we experience the pain. It is equally important to share our pain with others.

The third task of mourning is to adjust to our new environment. When we lose something close to us, our whole world seems to change. Part of our job is to recognize what we have lost, what our world is like since the loss, and how to deal with this new environment.

It is easier to withdraw, to pull into ourselves, than to face this new world. But if we shrink the scary environment of our grief, we will cease to grow. If we are able to see the world from a broader perspective, we will ultimately expand ourselves.

The fourth task of mourning is perhaps the hardest. It is to take the emotional energy we had invested in our loved one and reinvest it into something else. This is particularly difficult: we know that if we reinvest our energy, we may be setting ourselves up for another loss, which would mean more grief, more pain, and more work.

The divorcee will say, "Never again! Never EVER again, will I get married." Marriage means too much pain. It is easy to feel this way when a relationship ends in divorce. But the fact is, all relationships will end eventually.

All jobs will end. All health will end. All life will end. If we refuse to face these facts, we may never come to fully appreciate our relationships, our jobs, our health, or our lives.

When we lose something we love, we arrive at a better under-standing of the relationship we had with that person, place, or thing. This, in turn, brings us to a better understanding of our-selves. But understanding can only be accomplished though healthy grieving, and grieving takes work.

When we are confronted with a loss, we must accept the reali-ty of our loss, experience the fullness of our emotions, adjust to our new environment, and reinvest our energy in new relationships. Through reading, counseling, friends, grief groups, and prayer, we can gather the strength and support we need to work through our loss and grief.

Chapter Five

MYTHS OF GRIEF

If we or someone we care about experiences pain, it is natural to want to minimize that pain. But no matter how much we want to avoid it, no matter how compassionate our motives are, we are likely to do more harm than good by perpetuating the myths of grief.

Earlier, we attempted to define the word "death." We looked in the dictionary. We asked ourselves how we would know if somebody was dead. We examined society's feelings about death and grief.

Once again, I turn to the dictionary to define the term "myth." It reads, "A popular belief or tradition that has grown up around something." We all know that most popular myths are simply not true. When they are believed, they cause confusion, fear, pain, and misery.

Society perpetuates many myths about death. When we say that dead people have passed on or expired, we are continuing a myth. We do this because we feel powerless over death. If we can't conquer or control death, we will avoid it, withdraw from it, or deny it.

Death causes grief, and grief causes pain and suffering. We can work through this pain and overcome our suffering, but it requires hard work. It seems much easier to hide behind the false security of our myths. And the more people we can get to support us in hiding, the more power we believe we have over the truth.

The pain, suffering, and hard work that accompany grief cannot be avoided. By trying, all we do is create more problems, compounding the pain, suffering, and work that is necessary for us to grow.

Let's look at some of the myths of grief.

"Time will heal."

A terrible lie, and we hear it all the time. A widow stands tearfully in the back of the church. Inevitably, a well-intentioned friend walks up and says, "Don't worry, Jenny. Time will heal."

Can you tell me one thing that time has ever healed?

Does time heal a cut on your finger? Tomorrow morning, when you are slicing a bagel, cut your finger and don't do anything about it. Wait for time to heal it. Don't wash it. Don't put antiseptic, ointment, or a bandage on it. Don't give it any kind of care; just let time take its course. Will your cut heal?

If you walk to your car, stumble, and break your leg, do your friends walk by and say, "Yo, Fred! Nasty break, you got there—bones sticking out, blood gushing all over the pavement. Looks like you're in a lot of pain. Don't worry Fred, time will heal." That would be ridiculous.

Time will not heal a broken leg. Infection might set in. Gangrene could result. A person could die from a broken leg, if he or she waited for time to heal it. Yes, some bones can heal themselves, if they are left alone for some time. But a bone left to heal itself will seldom heal properly. A person could be disabled and quite possibly in pain for the rest of his or her life.

When you have a broken bone, someone has to work to get you to the hospital. Someone has to work to clean the wound, set the bone, immobilize the leg. After the patient works hard to stay off the broken leg, someone has to work to take off the cast. Then the patient may have weeks or months of strenuous physical therapy—more work.

What does it take to heal a broken leg or the pain of losing a loved one? Hard work. And after all that work, someone will say, "Boy, time sure healed that broken leg!" Not true! Hard work healed that broken leg.

While speaking in Michigan a few years ago, I asked my audience to name one thing that time heals. A man yelled out,

"Pregnancy!" Every woman looked at that man as he sank lower and lower in his chair, and then a woman shouted, "Labor healed that." Yes, labor. Any mother can tell you that labor is hard work.

Time won't heal grief. Hard work heals grief. The grieving have to work hard to identify their loss, their emotions, and who they are now that they've lost their loved one.

When you tell the bereaved that time will heal, the first question they ask is, "How much time?"

In our society we have what I call the thirteen-month wonder widow. Everyone tells her that in a year she'll be done with her pain and suffering, and she believes them. One year goes by, and the widow is not better; in fact, she's feeling worse. So the widow tells herself, "Thirty more days. I'll give it thirty more days, and then I'll be fine."

After about thirteen months of letting time heal their pain and suffering, these wonder widows come to my office ready to go to work on their grief. At grief groups you'll see them appear out of the woodwork. "It's been over a year and I know I should be all better, but I'm feeling worse." It's been one whole year and the only work they've done is pull sheets off the calendar.

It's the same with divorce. A lot of divorced people remarry as soon as that first year has passed. They think that after one year, it's okay for them to have intimate relationships again. Or now that one year has passed, they can go ahead and sell the house or kick the kids out or change jobs. It doesn't matter if they haven't worked to redefine themselves now that they're divorced. It doesn't matter if they have failed to gain new strengths and skills. As a result, many go on to repeat some of the same mistakes that led them to their painful divorce in the first place. They think one year should be enough time, and after that, they can get on with life.

Recovering alcoholics hear, "Don't make any important decisions during the first year of continuous sobriety. Wait until after a year, then you'll be better." Sometimes the first momentous decision a recovering alcoholic makes on his or her one-year anniversary is to go get drunk. For one whole year, the pain has been unbearable. The alcoholic has gone to meetings and listened to a lot of stories, but the pain hasn't gone away, because all he or she has been doing is collecting anniversary medallions at thirty days, three months, six months, one year. The alcoholic hasn't worked to redefine himself or herself after losing a beloved companion, alcohol.

"A year, and you'll be better; you'll be fine," is just not true. In a year, if you work hard. In six months, if you work hard. In a year and a half, if you work hard. It depends on what you had invested in what you lost and how hard you work to identify who you are now.

I know a woman whose husband killed their three children and then himself. In six months, the woman had processed most of her pain. She worked very hard at it. In fact, she spent four hours a week working through her pain in therapy. But her family couldn't accept her recovery. She wasn't supposed to be okay for a year or more. The entire family ostracized her and pushed her away because they thought she didn't grieve long enough. Who do you think had the most trouble working through their grief—the woman or her family?

If you truly want to help the grieving, don't say or believe that "time will heal." It is a myth. The fact is, only hard work heals. The bereaved need time to do their grief work, but time won't heal on its own.

"You'll get over it."

When you are grieving, you may often hear people say, "Don't worry. You'll get over it." This is another lie. The fact, is when you experience a loss in your life, you will never get over it. You will never be the person you were before the loss. You may work hard through your grief, but you will never be the same.

Do you recall the first love in your life, your first boyfriend or girlfriend? You probably still have memories, thoughts, and feelings for that person.

I was recently in Omaha, Nebraska, where I happened to see the person who had been the first love of my life. I recalled many of the feelings I had on our first date, our first kiss, our first . . . you get the idea. All those memories came back to me vividly. Imagine yourself at your high school reunion, seeing some of your friends again. When all the feelings come up into your throat, when the tears start to flow and you don't feel right because you thought you were over all those old relationships, don't worry. They are still an important part of who you are today.

For the widowed, years will pass and they'll eventually think they are over their loss. Then they will hear a song on the radio, or they will drive by that old, familiar restaurant, or they will glance at somebody walking down the street with that familiar jaunt. The pain will begin in the stomach and move up to the throat, the tears will flow, and they will think something is wrong with them, because they should be over their loss by now.

When you see people in this condition, tell them it's okay. Tell them they will never get over their loss. Let them know they are not going crazy. When someone who lost a father ten long years ago begins to cry as he talks about Dad, don't think there's something wrong with him. See those tears as genuine love, compassion, and pain. Give him your support, and love him.

The idea that you'll get over it is a myth. You can work hard through the grief, but you will never get over the loss.

"This is just a stage you're going through."

Some of us have read about the stages of grief and all the bullet points we will go through as we grieve. Not true. There are no stages of grief.

I have already stated that grief is the *process* of working through feelings that result from a loss. It is a process, not a program of step-by-step stages to recovery. If you believe that processing grief happens in stages, then it's easy to just sit around and wait for the next stage to come. People who expect stages to happen to them feel as if they have no control in their situation. When the stages never come, they feel even more helpless and hopeless than before.

If you believe the myth that grief comes in stages, then six months from now, when you again feel angry because of something you lost yesterday, you will think that you are regressing. "I'm going backwards! I'm not getting any better, I'm getting worse!" The fact is, you may have just recognized a new loss in your life. Every new loss brings new feelings, and you will have to do new work to redefine yourself.

Grief is a complex process that embodies a variety of feelings and behaviors. It is not a series of stages. In fact, as we work through grief, we may be at several different places in the process at once.

"True believers don't cry."

This is a myth you might hear when a loved one dies. The bereaved feel pain, and as a result of that pain, they mourn. The mourning comes in the form of tears. But at the funeral, the pastor or a parishioner might say, "No need to cry. If you are a true believer, this is a time of joyous celebration!"

The myth suggests that if you are a true believer, if you have faith, you don't have to grieve. If you cry when your loved one dies, then you have lost your faith as well as your loved one.

The next time you attend a Christian funeral and hear a priest or pastor say, "No need to cry, no need to mourn this death," I want you to stand right up and say, "Excuse me, pastor. . . ."

"Yes, what is it?"

"Excuse me, pastor, but I am confused."

"Well, what are you confused about, my dear?" (Clergy hate for people to be confused. They will clarify their point until the proverbial cows come home.)

"Pastor, what is the shortest sentence in the Bible?"

Few people at the funeral will know the answer, but the pastor will. The pastor will know that the shortest sentence in the Bible is John 11:35—Jesus wept.

Jesus wept at the loss of his dear friend Lazarus. This wasn't his dad, his mom, or his child, just his friend. And the kicker was, Jesus knew he'd get his friend back. Still, he felt his loss, and he wept.

As you sit back down in the pew, tell the pastor, "Well, that's what confuses me, pastor. Rumor has it that Jesus was a true believer." You won't make many friends this way, but you will get your point across. To mourn the loss of a loved one doesn't mean you lack faith. Crying is a natural, healthy response to grief.

It is not just at funerals that you are told, "True believers don't cry." You hear it all the time. Don't cry, you can always get another job, another spouse, another car, another whatever. "Don't cry" is just another way of saying, "Don't grieve."

"Anticipated grief is easier to handle."

This myth usually comes across through comments like "Long-term illness means short-term grief," or "Gee, you've known he was dying for six months. You should have been prepared for his death."

Sometimes it sounds like "You're lucky, your wife is dying of cancer. My wife left all of the sudden—heart attack. The family had no time to prepare for her death."

Remember the diagram of Sequential Reactions to Loss from page 87. Imagine this scenario: Ambulance staff drive like crazy to respond to a call from a private residence. When they arrive, a woman confronts them, "Where have you been? I called half an hour ago!" (Anger.)

The medics rush into the room where the woman's husband lies quietly. They detect a faint pulse and shallow breathing. "Looks like a stroke," one of the medics tells the other. The woman yells, "He didn't have a stroke! My God, he's only thirty-nine years old! Don't you guys even know how to do your job?" (Denial. More anger.)

The woman wants to ride in the ambulance to the hospital. She appears confused as she hurries to find the green shoes that go with her green purse. Her stomach is upset, she's trying to lock the dog in the basement, kids are crying in the other room—the woman appears very disorganized.

This woman is already feeling the loss of what was a healthy husband only moments before. She's experiencing emotions associated with that loss, and she mourns by displaying her emotions. In ignorance, one medic says to another, "Got a difficult woman here."

When the ambulance arrives at the hospital, the patient is rushed to the emergency room. The family gathers to wait, and the oldest son says, "What do you mean, I can't go in there and be with my dad? What kind of crazy rules do you have around here? I know the medic said stroke, but my dad couldn't have had a stroke. He was perfectly healthy this morning!" (Denial. Anger.)

The family waits. The men pace. The women huddle around the wife and cry. The family members are beginning to feel the loss of a healthy husband and father. One nurse says to another, "They're going to be a difficult group, so watch them—especially the wife."

The man is stabilized and taken to the Intensive Care Unit. Here, the family and hospital staff are once again at odds. Only one visitor at a time is allowed in the ICU, and for only five minutes every hour. The visitor may not touch the patient. So the wife visits her husband, but from a great emotional and physical distance.

In a matter of days the woman has the entire hospital staff upset. She's told the administration exactly what she thinks about the hospital's rules: "If I could spend fifty-five minutes with him every hour, instead of just five, he'd be better by now!" She's complained to the staff about her husband's care: "What do you mean, he can't even have plain water? You don't have to be a nurse to tell that he's thirsty." And she's complained to the doctor about her husband's illness: "If he didn't have to use a bedpan, if he could just get up and walk around a little, if he could just. . . ."

A few weeks go by and the man is moved to a private room. By now the wife is experiencing all kinds of physical symptoms, and she's seeing her doctor about stress. She's not going to work. Her everyday activities are all messed up. She's living out of a suitcase, sleeping in a chair in her husband's room. Her life is completely disorganized. Now the whole hospital staff is saying, "Whew! That's a difficult woman."

After a few more weeks in the hospital, the woman's husband dies. The doctor approaches her in the waiting room and says, "Mrs. Smith, I'm sorry. But your husband just passed away." The doctor cannot say "dead" or "died;" he'll say "expired," "didn't make it," or "passed away." And the woman will respond, "No! No! That can't be true! Yesterday, he was doing so well!" And when the doctor says, "I'm sorry. But there was nothing we could do," he has to watch his back. Some doctors have been hit, kicked, slapped, punched, and sworn at. When doctors tell survivors that a loved one has died, angry behavior is often directed at them.

So the woman will cry, and she will blame the hospital, the doctors, and the nurses. "Dumb hospital. Dumb nurses. I should never have brought him here in the first place. He was so healthy, so young. He had every reason to live, and no reason to die!" The wife will be disorganized, angry, and full of denial.

But now, instead of calling her a "difficult woman," hospital staff are supportive. The nurses put their arms around her. One gets her a sweater. Another calls her family and friends. Another gets her a cup of coffee, and so forth.

This woman displays some of the same behaviors she did before, but instead of getting a "D" for difficult, she gets a "G" for grieving. Because she is identified as grieving, the hospital staff comfort her. But this woman, along with every other family member, has been grieving from the very beginning. The grieving began when the ambulance took the man away from his home.

What did the woman lose when the medics first took her husband out of the house? She lost companionship. She lost her bed-partner. She lost the security of having a healthy husband. These are big losses. It stands to reason there was big grief.

What did the woman lose while her husband was in the emergency room? She lost control. Do you grieve when you lose control? You bet you do! She lost a sense of security. She no longer knew what was going on with her husband, or herself. She lost time with her spouse. These, too, are tremendous losses that result in tremendous grief.

In his room, the husband had wires connected to him, tubes coming out of his arms and his throat. He couldn't communicate well. He had to squeeze her hand once for yes, twice for no. Again, the woman experienced new and significant losses, which brought new and significant grief.

Weeks later, when the man died in his hospital bed, this woman lost her last hopes for his recovery. All of the earlier losses were compounded by her husband's death, and her grief became even larger.

With divorce you hear people say, "The hearing in court? Gonna be a breeze! Why, I kicked him out six months ago. It's been five months since I filed for divorce. The hearing only makes it all final. I knew our relationship was over long ago!" But when the judge slams the gavel on the bench and says, "Divorce granted," people faint. Their legs don't work. They forget where they parked their cars. They cry and they curse and they blame. And they say, "My God, I thought I was over this." People who have been through divorce will tell you, you're not divorced until you're divorced.

It's the same thing with death. A loved one is not dead until he or she is dead.

It could have been six weeks or six months since the medics took that man to the hospital. The death is only real now that the widow is at the funeral home. She's cries, caresses the body of her dead husband, and hugs family and friends. But some people will say, "For heaven's sake, look at her! I mean, it's been *six months*. She knew her husband was dying. And here she is, crying and act-ing up. No, don't put your arm around her, you'll just encourage her. Besides, she should be past this stage by now."

What does this woman lose at the funeral home? She loses denial. She can no longer deny the death of her husband. She loses the ability to communicate with her husband, no more hand squeezes, yes or no.

Two days later, her husband's body is lowered into the grave. What does she lose? The body of her husband. She's never going to see her loved one again. And later, there will be that first anniver-sary without her husband, that first holiday, that first birthday.

These are tremendous losses, and all mean tremendous grief. But in her mourning, people will suggest that she is acting weird, unbelievable, or in bad taste, because there was a long-term illness, and she had plenty of time to come to terms with her loss.

A few years ago I received a strange phone call in the middle of the night. I picked up the phone and a husky voice asked, "Is this the death man?"

Death man? I had been called worse things in my life, but death man was a first. I asked the caller what was on his mind, and he explained, "I just got off work and drove by my mom's house. I noticed the light was on, so I stopped. I found my mother crying. She said she'd been crying for two days! She hasn't slept. She hasn't eaten. She's just been crying. I don't know what to do!" I asked him what his mother was crying about, and he said, "I don't know. I didn't ask her. But Dad died six months ago. Maybe she's still upset about that."

I asked him to put his mom on the phone. I told her that her son said she'd been crying for two days. She said she had. "That sounds like a long time to be crying," I said. "What have you lost?"

This woman said that she woke up two mornings ago and realized for the first time that she couldn't remember the sound of her husband's voice anymore. Tremendous loss, tremendous grief.

Whenever you lose something, you will grieve. The woman lost the ability to recall her husband's voice. It was a major loss to her, causing major grief. Her son couldn't understand this because he thought she should be over her grief by now.

If you believe that anticipated grief is easier to handle, tell me why parents of kids with leukemia have such tremendous grief when their children die? There are often four, five, or six years of illness before their child's death. These parents have plenty of time to work through their grief, and yet, they grieve.

Another example can be found closer to home, in today's corporate culture. When a worker is given notice that his or her position will be cut in six months, we figure that the worker has plenty of time to grieve. "Gee, Bill, I don't know why you're so upset. You've known for six months that your job was being cut. How come you're crying in your beer now?"

When we tell someone that long-term anticipation of a loss makes grief easier to handle, we are perpetuating a lie. What's worse, by assuming that a survivor should have gotten over his or her grief, we are withholding our care and support from the bereaved. Instead, when someone we know thinks, "I must be crazy. I thought I'd be all grieved out by now," we must ask them what they just realized they have lost.

The idea that anticipated loss is easier to process than sudden, unexpected loss is a myth. In reality, a lingering illness before a death, or long-term notice before a loss, doesn't make that loss any easier to accept when it finally occurs.

"Death means only loss."

Another myth suggests that death means only loss, and grief will certainly follow that loss.

As a therapist, I administer a standard test that is designed to assess the emotional condition of my patients. The test is called the Minnesota Multiphasic Personality Inventory, or MMPI. I give my patients this inventory on their first visit to my office. Basically, this tool tells me how emotionally stable or unstable a patient is at that particular time.

The MMPI consists of more than 500 true-or-false questions. Test results are plotted on a graph that shows levels of depression, anxiety, nervousness, degree of honesty, introverted or extroverted characteristics, obsessive-compulsive feelings or behaviors, and so on. In the hands of a competent professional, this test is an important tool for therapists and patients alike.

During lectures I show my audience the results of an MMPI from a woman who came to see me for marriage counseling a couple of years ago. She brought her husband along and both took the MMPI.

The results of the woman's MMPI showed that she was depressed, anxious, fearful, disorganized, and very introverted. Her husband's MMPI hinted at the reason: he was one of the most angry, chauvinistic, mean, hateful, inhuman humans I had ever come across.

Even I had a hard time sitting in the same room with this man. After three sessions I found myself thinking, "When will this lady see the light? When will she see this man for all that he is, and leave this rotten relationship?" I'm a counselor, but I am also a human being. It was obvious that the best thing this woman could do was end her marriage. In most counseling situations, however, it is important for clients to identify and come to terms with their own perceptions of reality and the steps necessary for their recovery. So I remained objective, never letting my opinion be known to either patient.

Counseling was difficult for both of these people. The woman was coming to understand the man she had married, and the man was coming to terms with her growing awareness. As a result, he called off counseling and forbade his wife to ever see me again.

The woman telephoned me that following spring. She had been arguing with my secretary and was angry when I picked up the phone. I wasn't taking any new patients at the time, and she insisted that she needed to see me as soon as possible.

I imagined that this woman had finally made a decision about her insufferable marriage. Maybe there was hope after all! I offered to see her at the first available time on my calendar and asked if her husband would be coming in with her. She said, "Dick, didn't you hear? My husband died last February. He had a massive heart attack."

That was why she wanted to see me. "I know you do marriage counseling, but I also know you work with grief. And Dick, my grief just doesn't feel right."

When she came to my office, I gave her another MMPI. Her first MMPI showed her to be depressed, anxious, fearful, and disorganized. Now her MMPI showed her to be optimistic, self-confident, and calm.

So how did she spell relief? D-E-A-T-H.

When this woman lost her husband, she gained her mental health. She still experienced grief, but not so much for the husband. She grieved the loss of her mental illness, which she had carried all through her marriage. She lost that illness when her husband died.

We often feel grief when we give up an illness or an injury. For example, when I came back from Vietnam, I was on crutches. Everyone opened doors for me. People talked to me and asked me about my injury. They helped me up stairs, carried my groceries to my car, and even cautioned others of my approach. "Hey, move it up there! Got a man on crutches coming through!"

Even the parking attendant at my doctor's office helped me locate a convenient parking place. When the doctor said I could give up the crutches, I was quite pleased at first. But when I rode the elevator down to the lobby, no one said a word to me. No one opened any doors for me. No one asked what happened, or how I was doing, or wished me luck.

You may know people who have had trouble letting go of a physical illness. After doing all that work to process their grief and identify who they were when they were ill, they began to recover. But recovery meant they had to grieve all over again. They had to grieve the loss of their illness, and now they had to identify who they were when they were recovered. It took a lot of work.

After a spouse dies, many widows and widowers say, "I can finally eat the foods I want to eat. I can cook when I want to cook. I can go where I want, when I want." That doesn't mean they don't miss their spouse. They simply realize that even in the midst of loss there are gains, even when that loss is due to death.

When we perpetuate the myth that death means only loss, we expect people to feel only sadness, never happiness or relief. We need to help the grieving understand that it is not wrong to feel some gain at a time of loss. Otherwise, they will think there is something terribly wrong with them, which is not necessarily true.

"Gain means only happiness."

Because of this myth, new parents think they are crazy to feel sadness at the birth of a child. Yes, the couple gains a child, but what do they lose? Maybe freedom. Maybe privacy. Maybe their sense of economic security. Maybe each other. When you become a parent, you lose your parent—at least, everything that person used to be to you, including all of the attention he or she used to give just to you. A child is a big gain, but it brings big losses, too.

As we discussed earlier, if you were to win the multi-million-dollar-mega-bucks-bingo-lottery, your friends would expect you to feel only happiness. You would have financial security for the rest of your life. You could have a new house, new car, new lifestyle. Winning the lottery would be a big gain. But it could also be a big loss, because you might lose your job, your present lifestyle, and the security of knowing who your real friends are.

When speaking to a group of professional social workers, I once suggested that every member of my audience worked with people who were experiencing loss and grief. A young woman in the front row patiently raised her hand and rebutted my suggestion.

"You are wrong on that point. I don't work with people facing loss and grief. I work in adoption. With adoption, there is only happiness."

Adoption certainly represents great gain, but what about the losses? Research suggests that babies who are put up for adoption often suffer maternal deprivation. We must also consider the loss experienced by the mother or father who gives up his or her child for adoption. Or the loss that a couple feels when they adopt a son or daughter after having been childless for fifteen years. It simply isn't true that there is no loss in the process of adoption, even though people experience great gain as well.

"You aren't crazy. What you are feeling is normal."

When survivors talk about the feelings surrounding their loss, they often say, "I don't know, I just feel crazy!" Too often, our response is, "You aren't crazy! What you are feeling is quite normal." This, too, is a myth. The feelings people experience when they lose something important in their lives may very well seem crazy to those people.

When a loved one dies, the bereaved person will experience any number of feelings. Some of these feelings will be new. Some will be felt with more intensity than ever before. Certainly, the bereaved will have feelings he or she isn't prepared to deal with. Feelings may seem to come at all the wrong times (as if there were a right time). The sad feelings come when the bereaved expects feelings of happiness; contentment comes just when the bereaved can't imagine coping with another hour of pain. The widow still feels like part of a couple, but her husband no longer sits at the dinner table. The widower still feels one with his wife, but he climbs into bed alone at night. The divorcée feels both the joy of her new-found freedom and the sorrow of being alone, often at the same time. The man who recently lost his job imagines a world of opportunity, but at the same time feels like his world is collapsing all around him.

It *is* crazy. As the bereaved grieve their loss and face the task of redefining themselves, they feel pain and happiness, tears and laughter. The craziness they feel is part of the grieving process. It doesn't help us or others to deny that craziness. Crazy feelings are a sign that we are in the process of working to identify who we are now, as a result of our loss. If we accept our feelings as a normal part of working through grief, we can begin to see that this crazy time is not the time to be making major decisions. We will be able to see some of the rocks, boulders, and hazardous places in our lives.

"Survivors only grieve for the loss of the dead."

Another terrible myth suggests that for the most part, when a loved one dies, all of our grief is for that individual. Or in a divorce, when the kids move in with one parent, all they lose is the other parent. This is simply not true.

A family system—any relationship, for that matter—is like a mobile hanging over a baby's crib. The mobile hangs there, nice and balanced with all those little giraffes and lions and tigers suspended at different levels. When you remove just one of those animals, the whole mobile goes cater-whompus. All of the animals get tangled up in each other, and the mobile is a real mess.

It is the same with relationships. When dad dies, you might hear people say to the kids, "Well, you still have your mom." That's not entirely true. The kids may still have mom, but they will never have mom the way she used to be. When a parent dies, or when parents divorce, the kids lose both of their parents.

A few years ago, a six-year-old said to me, "You know, mommy isn't like mommy anymore. She used to pack my lunch everyday. She used to jam all kinds of things in there. I couldn't always eat it all. But now, since my dad moved away, some days she forgets to even pack my lunch. She used to play with us a lot and read to us almost every night. But she doesn't hardly do that anymore. She spends a lot of time at work now. I hardly ever see her." This child lost both parents when Mom and Dad got divorced. Dad moved away, so he lost his father, and Mom is not the same person she used to be.

It is the same with death. It doesn't matter if the relationship is based in family or friendship. It doesn't matter if the bereaved is forty years old or four years old. The reality is, when we lose someone close to us, the loss is not limited to that one person. It affects our relationships with others who have also experienced the loss.

Problems Associated with these Myths

You are already an expert on the myths of grief, and you know the added pain and suffering these myths can create. But let's review some of these problems in greater detail. Maybe, after we better understand the problems we create, we will understand why it is important to stop perpetuating these myths.

The myth:

"Time will heal."

The problems: Those who believe this myth will not do the work of grieving. They will seldom work to redefine themselves after a loss. Furthermore, the supportive network of family, friends, neighbors, and professionals will not put forth the work necessary to comfort the bereaved. This almost guarantees more isolation for the bereaved. If time heals, then everyone can just stand back and wait for time to heal.

The myth:

"You'll get over it."

The problems: When the bereaved recall sentimental feelings about their loss after two, five, or fifteen years, they think they are unhealthy or that they carry around unresolved grief. The bereaved don't want others to know about their unhealthiness, so they quit communicating their normal and natural everyday thoughts and feelings. This can, indeed, lead to unhealthiness. It will prevent them from telling others who they really are, and it may destroy or inhibit other intimate relationships.

A significant loss will affect us forever. After all, we are made up of every experience we have ever survived. If someone tells you he is a survivor of World War II, you get to know a little bit more about that person. If someone tells you she is the mother of twelve children, the wife of an alcoholic, or the sister of a man who committed suicide, you get to know that person better. Our lives are changed forever by the experiences we survive. And that change is often for the better. It is a part of what makes us who we are today.

The myth:

"This is just a stage you are going through."

The problems: This myth encourages feelings of helplessness. Those who believe it feel that grief happens *to* them; they think they have no power in their situation. If the bereaved are angry immediately after a loss and then again months later, they think they are regressing. Furthermore, people close to the bereaved often expect them to pass through stages of grief, which are thought to occur on their own. As a result, people who should be supporting the bereaved may never get involved in comforting them.

The myth:

"True believers don't cry."

The problems: If the bereaved feel they have been faithful to their God, but they cry anyway, they will feel that they've lost their faith as well as their loved one. Grief from multiple losses is more difficult to work through than grief from a single loss.

Furthermore, telling the bereaved that true believers don't cry will encourage them to withdraw from the religious community and deny themselves the social and spiritual support they so desperately need.

The myth:

"Anticipated grief is easier to handle."

The problems: This myth can cause the bereaved to think they are abnormal or emotionally unhealthy because they feel sadness and pain long after they should be "over" their grief. Furthermore, family and friends will be less supportive because they believe the bereaved should be all grieved out by now. When people believe this myth, they often do not realize the effect that grief will have on their work, their relationships, their concentration—on all aspects of their lives—for months or years after their loss.

The myths:

"Death means only loss. Gain means only happiness."

The problems: If you do not accept the fact that all loss means some gain, just as all gain means some loss, you will not be prepared for the mixed feelings that always come with a change in your life. You may feel unhealthy when positive or happy feelings enter your life after a loss. You may also feel unhealthy when negative or sad feelings come after a major gain in your life. The fact is, it's perfectly healthy to have mixed feelings.

The myth:

"You aren't crazy. What you are feeling is normal."

The problems: When the bereaved feel hurt and confused after a loss, they don't see these feelings as normal. When others assure that them that they *are* normal, the bereaved will not believe them. Instead of sharing their pain and suffering, they may withdraw; after all, they don't want others to know how crazy they feel. This could prevent the bereaved from working through their grief.

The myth:

"Survivors only grieve for the loss of the dead."

The problems: If the bereaved only recognize the loss of their loved one, and not all the losses that go along with it, they will be unprepared for the pain and suffering they will feels for months, even years later. Once again, the bereaved may feel they are not getting over their grief as fast as they should.

If family and friends of the bereaved fail to recognize all the different losses that accompany death, the bereaved can be left feeling alone and misunderstood. Remember, if a child loses a father to death, the child also loses the person his or her mother used to be.

When we perpetuate myths about grief, we prolong the grieving process and cause more pain and suffering for the bereaved. We must work diligently to eradicate these myths, reminding ourselves to stop saying them out loud and to challenge others who perpetuate them. When we do, we will reduce needless suffering and allow ourselves and others to get on with the task of working through grief.

Chapter Six

THE FUNERAL

At some point, we may find ourselves planning a funeral for a family member or dear friend. When that day comes, we will likely be unprepared for the work that goes into this important ritual.

It is important to keep in mind that the funeral is more than just a ceremony for the dead. It is a tool to help the survivors begin to heal, and it is worth doing right.

History of Funerals

Many people believe that the only reason we have funerals is to make money for funeral directors. It is true that caring for the dead has become a major business. But throughout history, funerals have been a significant part of life. To the best of my knowledge, every society, culture, tribe, or group has had some kind of ritual to memorialize, spiritualize, or finalize the life of an individual who has died.

Some of us have witnessed funerals with less than five people in attendance, and most have seen funerals on television that drew millions of mourners. All of us have been to a funeral or can expect to attend one in the future.

Some people have the impression that all funerals are religious, but this is not the case. Some funerals are political. Others provide a time for quiet meditation, social reconstruction, reflection—whatever the survivors require.

Many people have the mistaken idea that funerals are for the deceased. In fact, funerals are for the living—they always have been and always will be. All the sociological, psychological, and spiritual needs that a funeral addresses are designed to meet the needs of the survivors. The needs of the dead have already been met. There may be offerings or prayers for the dead, of course, but even these are really made for the living. We must keep all the survivors in mind when we plan a funeral.

The funeral is a rite of incorporation, a ceremony whereby survivors move the deceased from the world of the living to the world of the dead. It is an opportunity for survivors' to acknowledge the death and use this process to meet their sociological, psychological, and spiritual needs.

Brief Therapy

In our society, the funeral ritual usually begins when survivors make the funeral arrangements. It generally concludes with the committal at a cemetery or the gathering of family and friends after the committal. The entire ritual may last only two or three days. This is rarely enough time for survivors to begin their healing process.

In the past, funeral rituals were brief because society needed to rid itself of the dead body before it became a health hazard. Today, with the modern sciences of embalming and preservation, we no longer need to make instant funeral arrangements. The deceased will be dead for a long time, and the needs of the survivors can take priority.

The survivors' grief won't end after two or three days; it can take months, even years. A brief funeral marks the beginning of the grieving process.

Grief Therapy

Grief therapy is the process of assisting others as they work to identify themselves after a significant loss. The funeral is an important part of this. It should be regarded as a selfish affair: an opportunity for survivors to focus on their grief, pain, and need to reorganize themselves.

The work of grief is personal and individual. In order to meet the needs of the survivors, the funeral should be personal and individual as well. When arranging a funeral, survivors make decisions that will affect their grief for the rest of their lives.

Group Therapy

The funeral is a form of group therapy. Like any group therapy, it must address the needs of the group, as well as the needs of individual members within that group.

Numerous groups are affected when an individual dies. There is the family group: mother, father, sister, brother, grandchildren, parents. There are also friendship groups, working groups, religious groups, social groups, and political groups. All of these groups have needs that must be met. Each should be informed of the death so they can make plans to meet their common or individual needs.

Within these groups are still smaller groups. For example, a family group might consist of children, elderly relatives, and middle-aged adults. A religious group might encompass an entire congregation, as well as a group of choir members or elders. The funeral should meet the needs of all of them.

Reality Therapy

Reality therapy encourages patients to face the reality of their situation head-on. The funeral is an excellent tool for this. At the funeral home, where the body is present and survivors are constantly talking about the deceased, it's hard to deny the reality of the death. The loss begins to sink in, and survivors come to realize that the person really is dead.

The Parts of a Funeral

The funeral can gently bring survivors to the full awareness of their loss. Calling the funeral director, completing funeral arrangements, visiting with others at the funeral home, confronting the dead body, attending the ceremony, going in procession to the grave site, driving out of the cemetery—each of these makes the reality of the death that much more real.

Obituary

The obituary, or death notice, reports a death in the community. It is posted in a newspaper or delivered over a local radio station. When you think about it, an obituary is an S.O.S., a plea for help from the survivors.

The obituary first lists the name of the person who died, followed by the names of surviving family members. After that, the obituary says, in essence, "We the survivors, who have lost big, need your handshakes, hugs, kisses, and comfort. Therefore, we will be at such-and-such place at such-and-such time."

The obituary is a blatant call for help. We should always scan the obituaries for survivors who need us to comfort them in their time of pain and suffering.

Funeral Arrangements

Funeral arrangements are usually made by immediate family members. The act of planning a funeral brings closure to the life of the loved one, helps survivors come to terms with the death, and allows the family to begin redefining itself.

If the deceased was the leader of the family, the rest of the family might shift, manipulating each other in his or her absence. Families sometimes determine the new leader by taking indirect polls or finding issues to fight over. I've seen families fight over the color of the casket, the music to be played, and the amount of money to be spent. Although this seems to be traumatic and often irreverent, it's a good beginning for the restructuring process that must occur.

Register Book

No one is invited to a funeral, but everyone is expected to attend. The register book is an opportunity to sign in so that, at a later date, the survivors can see that you attended.

The funeral is a busy time for survivors. They are more occupied with their grief than with who came and who didn't. Later, many survivors can't remember the hundreds of people who came to comfort them at their time of loss, but they cannot forget the one or two who failed to attend the funeral. The register book provides a record of one's attendance.

Viewing the Body

Many people say, "I'm not going to view the body. I want to remember him the way he was."

I know how important it is to remember others as they were. But it is equally important to remember them for who they are now. When people die, they are no longer who they were. They are dead.

When a body is placed in an open casket, it becomes a place for the bereaved to gather and receive support. It can help initiate their grief. I have seen people yell at the body of their loved one. I have seen them slap, kiss, or demand a response from the deceased. Of course, the dead cannot respond, but this lack of response tells survivors that the death is real. When they see the body, they know that person is really dead.

Viewing the body helps survivors bring closure to the relationship they had with their loved one. Closure may come in the form of prayer. It may be a message to the deceased that was never given while he or she was alive. It might be a pat or a kiss, as if to say, "This is the end." Survivors no longer need to ask the question, "Where is this person now, in my life?" The reality is before them.

Some would argue that viewing the body is unnatural, because clothing and cosmetics are applied. They believe that clothing and cosmetics are a denial of the reality of death. But almost all living bodies wear some cosmetics. If you are skeptical, let me remind you that you probably are wearing deodorant right now. This may be a denial of life, but for the most part, it makes us more acceptable to others. This is the purpose of using clothing and cosmetics on a dead body—it makes the body more acceptable to the living. A body that is clean and positioned in a way that suggests no pain or suffering is easier to be around, identify with, touch, and accept.

Viewing the body also allows survivors to stop searching. Soldiers who are missing in action remind us how important it is to find the dead and accept that their death is real. By seeing and touching the body, our search can come to an end.

Organization and Direction

When a person suffers a loss, he or she feels disorganized for a time. According to Dr. Paul Irion, a funeral is an organized, purposeful, group-centered, time-limited response to a loss. This is why funeral directors are called "directors"—they give direction at a time when the bereaved need it most. This direction aids survivors as they work to process the pain of their grief.

Many funerals are organized from a religious or spiritual standpoint. Almost all religions have some plan, procedure, ritual, or ceremony to follow after a death. Again, such activities bring organization to the bereaved at a time when they feel terribly disorganized. Friends, neighbors, coworkers, and others also provide organized support at funerals. I can't begin to tell you how many widows I know who, in their deepest hour of sorrow and disorganization, were grateful to be able to make organized decisions with the help of professionals, friends, and family members. The funeral taught them them that they would be able to make organized decisions in the future.

Professional Involvement

Professionals support the survivors throughout the process of planning, arranging, directing, and officiating at funerals. In the past, these professionals consisted only of clergy and funeral directors. Today, they also include nurses, physicians, hospital chaplains, social workers, and volunteers who work in oncology, long-term care, and hospice.

During the funeral, these professionals have enough contact with the survivors to see where they are in the grief process. They can provide valuable support to the bereaved, assisting the whole family as it works to redefine itself and helping individual family member to process their grief.

Funeral directors, clergy, hospice volunteers, and social workers can provide additional support to survivors by following up with them after the funeral. The bereaved often stop ritualizing their grief once the funeral is over, and this puts their healing in jeopardy. Professionals can help them create other rituals and ceremonies to assist them over the vacant weeks and months that follow the funeral.

The Processional

The processional, or cortege, is the physical process of moving a body from the world of the living to the world of the dead. The processional often starts at a funeral home, moves to a place of worship, then proceeds to the cemetery. This procession shows the community that a death has occurred, a death that has affected a number of people. It also reminds the community that death is a constant reality of life.

The procession is as important to the survivors as it is to the larger community. Survivors are overwhelmed by the tragedy and pain of their loss, and they often feel that their own life has ended. But as the procession moves slowly through the streets, communities, and neighborhoods on the way to the cemetery, survivors are reminded that the world continues. Even in the throes of their grief, life goes on.

The processional is also beneficial from a safety standpoint. Grief is a period of preoccupation, disorganization, and confused thinking for the bereaved. It's a bad time to place these individuals behind the wheel of a car without direction and guidance. The processional, in its organized and safety-conscious manner, moves the bereaved safely to their destination.

Committal Rites

Committal rites usually take place whether the body is cremated, buried in a cemetery, or donated to a school of medical science. It not only allows survivors to come to grips with the finality of the death, it also brings together a group of people who can support the survivors in their time of grief.

Donation or cremation of the body does not preclude a committal ceremony. Services can be carried out at the place of cremation or donation. Such services can comfort survivors well into the future by giving them a place to go when they feel a need to search for their deceased loved one.

Post-Funeral Gathering

After the committal rites, survivors often assemble at a place of worship, a family member's home, or other meeting place. Family members share food and drink, reminiscing with other survivors about the deceased. Sometimes survivors get upset because people talk about the humorous experiences they shared with the deceased. In fact, merry-making is a sign that the funeral has done its job. When grief has been processed in a healthy fashion, survivors are able to share more joyous occasions. Old relationships are reexamined, old memories retold, and reorganization can begin.

Cost

Funerals can cost anywhere from a few hundred to several thousand dollars, depending on the family's wishes. A funeral that costs several thousand dollars, but does not provide for family members—no viewing of the body, no processional or committal rites, no final gathering of the family—would probably be a waste of money. On the other hand, a much less expensive funeral that includes all of the above could be of tremendous value.

Funerals, whether simple or elaborate, often reflect the lifestyle of the deceased—and of the survivors. People living in poverty seldom have extremely expensive funerals, and those who are rich rarely have inexpensive funerals. The stereotypes of a funeral director gouging poor widows out of their money is simply not accurate. Funeral directors cannot repossess their merchandise after a burial. It would make no sense for them to encourage survivors to spend money they do not have.

The average cost of a funeral today runs about $3,000. If 150 people attend the funeral, the average cost per person is $20. Since the funeral is designed to meet the needs of all survivors, you can see how cost-effective this period of brief-grief-group-reality therapy really is. In the long run, it's cheaper to make the most of this therapeutic tool, when you compare it to seeing a professional grief therapist at $90 per hour. On the other hand, if the funeral doesn't meet the needs of the survivors, it doesn't matter how much it costs: it will have been a waste of money.

I have worked for over twenty years in grief and bereavement counseling. I have seen many people blunder when they try to cut corners with the funeral service. Whenever this happens, it almost always comes back to haunt them. In the long run, it increases their chances of unresolved grief and their need to seek professional counseling. I encourage people to use the funeral for all it's worth—it is an essential tool for helping the bereaved resolve their grief.

The needs of the survivors are constantly changing. If a funeral is planned ahead, especially by someone anticipating his or her own death, the needs of the survivors are often ignored. I don't mean to suggest that families shouldn't put money aside to cover the expenses of a funeral—that is a prudent idea. But preplanning a funeral doesn't always take into account the needs of the survivors. After all, the funeral isn't for the deceased. The dead do not care about the color of the casket or the selection of music played during visitation. The funeral is for the survivors.

A healthy funeral wets the eyes, cleansing the survivors so they can begin that long, arduous process of redefining themselves. It should provide a safe environment for all survivors to express their pain and sorrow, as well as their hope and joy.

The funeral is a ritual that must be planned and conducted with a great deal of care for the survivors. If done properly, it will help them realize that their lives go on. The healing will begin.

THE END, THE BEGINNING

The preceding pages have been filled with words—black dots of ink on paper. Your eyes have read these words, and your brain has interpreted them according to your life experiences. Some of the same words that brought you feelings of sadness brought other readers feelings of joy or hope. As you work to redefine yourself after a loss, the stimuli that caused you pain yesterday may give you renewed hope tomorrow.

Perhaps you should put this book down for now and mark your calendar for ninety days from today. On that day, go back and re-read some of these same black dots of ink and see how far you've come.

After all, it is your life.

And you are a survivor.

Bibliography

Heinlein, Susan, Grace Brumett, and Jane Tibbals, eds. *When a Lifemate Dies: Stories of Love, Loss, and Healing.* Fairview Press: Minneapolis, 1997.

Holmes and Machoeski. "The Social Readjustment Scale." *Journal of Psychosomatic Research.* April 1967: 213-218.

Irion, Paul. *The Funeral: Vestige or Value?* Abingdon Press: Nashville, 1966.

Kübler-Ross, Elisabeth, M.D. *On Death and Dying.* MacMillan: New York, 1974.

Kushner, Harold S. *When Bad Things Happen to Good People.* Schocken Books: New York, 1981.

Levang, Elizabeth, Ph.D., and Sherokee Ilse. *Remembering with Love: Messages of Hope for the First Year of Grieving and Beyond.* Fairview Press: Minneapolis, 1992.

Parkes, Collin. *Bereavement: Studies of Grief in Adult Life.* International Universities Press: New York, 1973.

Worden, James. *Grief Counseling and Grief Therapy.* Springer Publishing Co.: New York, 1982.

Richard J. Obershaw, MSW, LICSW, holds degrees in psychology, mortuary science, and social work. He is the founder and director of The Grief Center and Burnsville Counseling Clinic in Burnsville, Minnesota, where he has a full-time private psychotherapy practice and serves as clinic administrator. A popular speaker, Mr. Obershaw travels and lectures across the United States and Canada to professional, corporate, and lay groups on the topics of death, grief, stress, personality issues, and other related topics. He lives in Burnsville, Minnesota.